The
Holy Sacrifice
of the Mass

A Search for an Acceptable Notion of Sacrifice

Michael McGuckian, SJ

HillenbrandBooks   GRACEWING

First published in 2005
jointly by

Gracewing Publishing
2 Southern Avenue
Leominster
Herefordshire HR6 0QF
England

Liturgy Training Publications
Archdiocese of Chicago
1800 North Hermitage Avenue
Chicago IL 60622-1101
USA

Published in the USA and Canada by Liturgy Training Publications under the imprint Hillenbrand Books. The imprint is focused on contemporary and classical theological thought concerning the liturgy of the Catholic Church. Further information available from the University of St. Mary of the Lake/Mundelein Seminary, 1000 East Maple Avenue, Mundelein IL 60060. litinst@usml.edu

UK ISBN 0-85244-634-9
USA ISBN 1-59525-007-7 HSCMS
Library of Congress Control Number: 2004117532

Cover art © The Crosiers/Gene Plaisted, osc

Printed in the United States of America.

Contents

Abbreviations

AAS   *Acta Apostolicae Sedis*

CCL   *Corpus christianorum, series Latina*

CSEL   *Corpus scriptorum ecclesiasticorum latinorum*

CT   *Concilium Tridentinum*

DS   Denzinger-Schömetzer, *Enchiridion Symbolorum*

DTC   *Dictionnaire de théologie catholique*

LNPNF   *A Select Library of the Nicene and Post-Nicene Fathers*

ND   Neuner-DuPuis, *The Christian Faith*

PG   *Patrologia Graeca*

PL   *Patrologia Latina*

SC   *Sources Chrétiennes*

Foreword

The Second Vatican Council's Constitution on the Sacred Liturgy said that in the Eucharist, followers of Christ participate in a celebration that is both sacrifice and communal meal. In recent decades we have tended to emphasize the meal dimension over the sacrificial aspect of Mass.

In part, this may explain Pope John Paul's stress on the Mass as a sacrifice in his recent encyclical *Ecclesia de Eucharistia,* "The Church of the Eucharist."

In this brief but wide-ranging book, Father Michael McGuckian explains that the concept of the Eucharist as a sacrifice has long posed difficulties for the Church, especially since the Reformation.

At the beginning of the sixteenth century, some bishops had difficulty with the notion of sacrifice and even opposed it. The Council of Trent resolved the question by asserting that the Mass was truly a sacrifice. But the question goes back to Saint Thomas Aquinas or earlier.

With Father McGuckian's help, one comes to see that discomfort with sacrificial language may derive from what he calls a "one-stage" manner of envisaging the Mass, one that focuses only on the death of Christ.

Instead, he proposes a "three-stage" conception of what takes place in the Eucharist, focusing also on the celebration of the Risen Lord's presence and anticipation of the heavenly banquet. His tripartite conception gives renewed importance to the Offertory, the Eucharistic Prayer, and the reception of Holy Communion.

Exploring Scripture, the Church Fathers, and historical developments, including postconciliar modifications of the Order of Mass, this brief volume offers much food for thought. In this Year of the Eucharist, I am pleased to commend it to all who wish to deepen their understanding of Holy Mass.

Most Reverend Terrence Prendergast, SJ
Archbishop of Halifax (Canada)
First Sunday of Advent
November 28, 2004

Preface

How is the Mass a sacrifice? That is the question to which this little book attempts to provide an answer. The question was first formulated in the early twelfth century by Peter Lombard, and his answer was one that has stood the test of time. He said that the Mass is a sacrifice because it is a memorial of the Sacrifice of the Cross, and that answer has adherents still. However, Catholic theology has ever maintained, as the Council of Trent put it, that the Mass is a "true and proper" sacrifice, in its own right. But the question remains: How? The Protestant theologians taunted the Catholics because they had no answer to that question. How can Catholics maintain so adamantly that the Mass is a sacrifice, if they do not know what a sacrifice is? In post-Tridentine Catholic theology there ensued a concerted effort to answer the question, but no satisfactory answer has yet been found.

The suggestion to be made here is that the proper notion of sacrifice was unearthed at the end of the nineteenth and the beginning of the twentieth century by scholars studying the nature of sacrifice in the Old Testament and in the surrounding Semitic and Greco-Roman cultures. One school of interpretation holds that in those traditional cultures, a sacrifice was a joyful meal celebrated in the presence of God and in His honor. In this book the attempt is made to see if that notion of sacrifice fits the Eucharist.

Doing that means challenging certain theses currently in possession in different areas. Against the current consensus in liturgical studies, it is necessary to maintain that the Offertory of the Mass is indeed a true offertory and not simply the preparation of the gifts. It is also necessary to show that the Last Supper, the first Mass, was also a "true and proper" sacrifice. One area where the most startling results emerged has been in applying this model of sacrifice to the Sacrifice of the Cross, because if the model is to work it has to fit all the facts.

Much of what is within is of necessity superficial. The focus has been kept strictly on the fundamental question, and possible developments must be left to another day. If, however, the argument is deemed to be successful, a chapter of Eucharistic theology will be closed which has remained unfinished for a very long time.

In quoting from the scriptures, I have used both the Jerusalem Bible and the Revised Standard Version, except in a few cases where I provided my own translation. Then I have given the original word along with a translation that I believe captures most accurately the relevant nuances of the original language.

I would like to thank a number of people who have contributed to this project. First of all, I wish to thank my Jesuit superiors who made it possible for me to do work of this kind. More immediately, I wish to thank the staff and seminarians of St. Peter's Major Seminary, Zomba, Malawi, where I gave the lectures on the Eucharist that focused this question for me. Further, I wish to thank the Jesuit communities of Milltown Park, Dublin, and the Gregorian University, Rome, in whose libraries I found the answer presented here. I wish to thank my brother, Rev. Alan McGuckian, sj, who helped so much to see the manuscript through to publication. Finally, I wish to dedicate this book to my mother and the memory of my father.

Michael C. McGuckian, sj
February 15, 2002
Feast of Saint Claude la Colombière, sj

Chapter 1

A "True and Proper" Sacrifice

The Catholic Church believes and teaches that "[t]he Eucharist is above all else a sacrifice."[1] In the light of that, it is a strange situation for Catholic theology that we do not know clearly what a sacrifice is. Of course, we must have some idea of sacrifice, however vague, in order for the affirmation to have any meaning at all, but no concept of sacrifice has yet been worked out that meets with general acceptance. Does this not mean that we do not really know what we are talking about when we affirm that the Eucharist is a sacrifice? And does it not also mean that we do not really know what we are doing when we celebrate the Eucharist? We follow the rubrics of the Mass more or less carefully, but have we a real idea of what is going on?

The basic problem is that we have no experience of sacrifice on which to base a concept. Indeed, this lacuna is widely recognized. Hans Küng has remarked: "Since in modern man's environment cultic sacrifices are no longer offered, . . . the concept of sacrifice is not related to any experience and has thus become largely misleading and unintelligible."[2] And another commentator has pointed out: "In contemporary sophisticated societies, talk of sacrifice can easily seem primitive and alien. One wonders how many people in our Eucharistic congregations really intend to *sacrifice*."[3] One must indeed wonder. But, if the Eucharist is "above all else a sacrifice," and we are not sacrificing at the Eucharist, then something is fundamentally wrong.

It is not that the effort has not been made to work out a concept of sacrifice. A concerted effort was embarked upon in the wake of the Protestant Reformation to solve the problem, but it has failed. As one recent author put it: "In our own day, at the close of the second millennium, the situation which has obtained from the thirteenth to the twentieth century in the matter of the theology of Eucharistic sacrifice remains unresolved."[4]

THE BACKGROUND

Our present predicament has been a long time in the making. Up until the Reformation the sacrificial quality of the Eucharist was simply taken for granted in the Christian tradition. During the first millennium, sacrifice remained a commonplace aspect of the surrounding culture and everyone knew by experience what a sacrifice was. When Christendom was established throughout Europe, the practice of other sacrifices ceased, and gradually the experiential concept of a sacrifice, apart from the Eucharist itself, faded away. It was only in the twelfth century, with Peter Lombard, that anyone thought to ask the question, How is the Eucharist a sacrifice? And Lombard's answer was: "We may briefly reply that what is offered and consecrated by the priest is called a sacrifice and an immolation because it is a memorial and a representation of the true sacrifice and holy immolation made upon the altar of the Cross" (*Sentences*, IV, dist. 12, cap. 5.).

This answer is clearly unsatisfactory. It is simply not true to say that because the Eucharist is a memorial and a representation of the Sacrifice of the Cross that it is itself, therefore, a sacrifice. The concept of a memorial does not include the re-enactment of the reality remembered. A memorial of a victory in war may be a statue of the general who won the war or a garden of remembrance for the soldiers who died in the war, but the one thing it cannot be is a victory in a war. What is clear from the answer that he gave is that Lombard had no idea what a sacrifice is. He made no suggestion at all as to how the Eucharist might be a sacrifice in its own right. No one saw this as a problem at the time, or for a long time to come. From the thirteenth to the sixteenth century, Lombard's *Sentences* continued to be the manual of theological study, and during those three centuries, while commenting on the *Sentences* was the standard task of every doctor of theology, none of them commented on the 12th Distinction of Book IV, which deals with the Eucharist as a sacrifice. The important question in Eucharistic theology all during that period was the real presence and transubstantiation. The sacrificial character of the Eucharist was quite taken for granted, and the issue was only treated in passing in connection with related questions.[5] "It was enough for them that the unanimous teaching of Christian antiquity, interpreting the text of scripture, regarded the Eucharist as the unbloody sacrifice of the new law."[6]

It is not surprising, then, that when Luther began the attack on the sacrifice of the Mass, Catholic theology was not well prepared to meet it. Francis Clark tells the story succinctly and well.

> The first generation of Catholic apologists . . . continued this traditional method. As the years passed, however, there grew a demand for a more rigorously scientific argument to meet the challenge of the Reformers. In his *Apology for the Confession of Augsburg* in 1531 Philip Melanchton taunted the Romanists with failing to give a definition of sacrifice. While they poured out a spate of books to assert that the Mass is a sacrifice, he said, not one of them had defined their basic term. Under the pressure of these controversies some of the Catholic theologians began to take up the challenge on the ground chosen by their opponents. The traditional explanation of the pre-Reformation theology, that the Eucharist was truly a sacrifice because it was the sacramental representation and offering of the sacrifice of the Cross, seemed to them too weak; it seemed to give an opening for the Reformers to retort: "We agree that the Eucharist commemorates the one past sacrifice, and for that very reason we argue that it cannot be itself a sacrifice." Adequately to refute this objection it seemed necessary to work out a strict metaphysical definition of sacrifice and then apply it to the Mass. Cardinal Gaspar Contarini (d. 1542): "It is vain that we shall try to give an account of our sacrifice unless we first understand what sacrifice is—a point, I see, about which many of those who so often discourse about our Mass-sacrifice are in the dark. I have found few authors who have given a good explanation in their writings of what sacrifice is." Melchior Cano: "If there has ever been a dispute in which it is necessary to define what it is all about, I am very sure it is this." Matthew Galenus . . . referred to "the inextricable labyrinth of the attempt to find a definition of sacrifice in the proper sense."[7]

The effort to find an adequate concept of sacrifice has continued for more than four centuries now, and has still not met with success. That failure, however, cannot be accepted as terminal. The effort to uncover the truth about sacrifice must continue, for the urgency is as great now as it was four centuries ago. There is no single concept more important for Christian theology than that of sacrifice. And it is not simply a matter of the theology of the Eucharist. The concept of sacrifice is central to the whole vision of faith. The Eucharist makes the Church, and the Eucharist is a sacrifice, so, if we do not understand sacrifice we do not understand the Eucharist and we do not understand the Church. The Second Vatican Council teaches us that "[t]aking part in the Eucharistic sacrifice, the source and summit of the whole Christian life, [Christians] offer the divine victim to God, and themselves along with him" (*Lumen Gentium,* 11). And Saint Augustine understood the whole mystery of salvation as our sharing in the universal sacrifice, which is the whole community of the redeemed offered to God by their High Priest (*De civitate Dei* 10, 6: PL 41, 284). These quotations indicate that sacrifice is a concept necessary for the understanding of the overall shape of the Christian vocation. The concept also has ramifications throughout the range of sacramental theology. To take only the most obvious example, the problem of the crisis in priestly identity is immediately connected to the lack of a concept of sacrifice, for without an understanding of sacrifice there can be no understanding of priesthood, the two concepts being co-relative, a priest (*sacerdos, hiereus*) being a man who offers sacrifice.

A PURELY SACRAMENTAL SACRIFICE?

The need of this concept could not possibly be greater, and it is in this context that this book seeks to be placed. It is the purpose of this book to suggest that the concept of sacrifice which theology needs and has been searching for these last four centuries is now available. In fact, it has been available for at least the best part of a century already, but has not so far been put to its proper use. The reason for that lack of interest is connected with a change in the Catholic theology of the Eucharist during the twentieth century which must be discussed in order to justify the project as a reasonable effort at all, since during the past century the conclusion has begun to be drawn that the quest for a concept of sacrifice is futile, if not completely wrong-headed altogether. As Karl Rahner pointed out some time ago: "In recent theological writing it has been emphasized that it is incorrect or at least inadequate to assume as starting point for reflection on sacrifice in Christianity any idea of sacrifice belonging to the Old Testament or derived from comparative religion, and to demand that this concept must be exemplified in the sacrifice of the Cross or of the Mass. . . ."[8] This opinion, that a concept of sacrifice is not necessary to the understanding of the Eucharist, is justified on the basis that it is sufficient to assert that the Eucharist is a sacrament of the Sacrifice of the Cross. In that case, it is argued, whatever it is in the Cross that constitutes it as a sacrifice will be verified also in the case of the Eucharist by the power of the sacrament.

This is a new version of Lombard's first answer to the question. He said that the Eucharist is a sacrifice because it is a memorial and a representation of the Sacrifice of the Cross. Now it is said that the Eucharist is a sacrifice because it is a sacrament of the Sacrifice of the Cross. This new version is, indeed, better than the old one. The concept of a memorial does not contain the re-enactment of the reality remembered, but the concept of a sacrament does contain the reality signified. It is, therefore, true to say that the Eucharist is a sacrifice because it is a sacrament of the Sacrifice of the Cross, and this point is essential to the theology of the Eucharist. There is no doubt that the understanding of the Eucharist as a sacramental sacrifice is perfectly valid in what it affirms; the problem is in what its current exponents take it to deny.

That the Eucharist is a sacramental sacrifice is beyond dispute. It has always been the teaching of the Tradition that in the Eucharist we offer the Sacrifice of the Cross sacramentally. Today, however, some are taking the further step and saying that it is a sacrifice *only* because it is a sacrament of the Sacrifice of the Cross, that it is a *purely* sacramental sacrifice, and not a sacrifice in its own right. One early exponent of this approach, Dom Anscar Vonier, considered the denial of the natural sacrifice to be essential to his understanding of the sacramental sacrifice. "It is of utmost importance, in order to safeguard the sacramentality of the sacrifice of the Mass, to eliminate from it all such things as would make it into a natural sacrifice, a human act, with human sensations and human circumstances."[9] And this opinion of Vonier seems to have gained many adherents. In his recent general review of Eucharistic theology, Edward Kilmartin proposed a judgment which seems to be widely shared. "The problem with all theologies of the Mass of the post-Reformation period originates in the search for the grounds of sacrifice in the rite itself, and not in the representation of the Sacrifice of the Cross. Catholic theology did not take seriously enough the fact that 'sacrifice' in the history-of-religions sense was

abolished with the Christ-event."[10] Now, if this is true, then there
is indeed no point in trying to work out how the Mass is a sacrifice,
because, on this view, the Eucharist is not a sacrifice in the normal
sense of the word at all. However, not all Catholic theologians have
accepted this conclusion. Karl Rahner disputed it on a couple of
grounds. He made the epistemological point that a word used in any
intelligent discourse must have a meaning. "Consequently, if the
sources of revelation call the death on the Cross or the Mass a sacrifice,
they must employ a term which has at least a generally defined sense
and content independent of its use in this instance. Otherwise they
would only be putting a verbal label on an occurrence already understood
without it."[11] And he further disputed the assertion that the Eucharist
is not a sacrifice in the ordinary sense of the word on the basis of
the traditional faith of the Church.

We know from the teaching of the Church that the liturgical
proceeding which we call the Mass is a *sacrificium visible* (D 1740).
This obviously states and means that the visible ritual action itself
is a sacrifice. It cannot merely be the visible manifestation of a sacrifice
which in itself is invisible. It is not the case that under or behind the
visible ritual proceeding which is not itself a sacrifice (a mere meal, for
example, or a celebration of the mysteries), something is present in
a hidden way, and this is what can be called the sacrifice. A correct
interpretation of the doctrine of the Council of Trent regarding the
sacrificium visibile of the Mass must maintain that the sacrificial character
of the Mass is to be sought on the plane of the visible liturgical action.[12]

On this basis, Karl Rahner reached the methodological
conclusion which we hope to confirm here: "As far as method is concerned, therefore, we can and must start from the usual concept of
sacrifice (or at least from those elements of it which are generally
acknowledged to belong to a sacrifice), in the way that has been custom-
ary in the theology of the last few centuries."[13]

The One Sacrifice of Christ

Karl Rahner maintained that the teaching of the Church "obviously
states and means that the visible ritual action itself is a sacrifice." And
yet Vonier believed that he had to deny it, and his reason was a serious
one. According to him, the denial of the sacrifice on the level of the

visible ritual action is demanded by the unicity of the Sacrifice of
the Cross. "If the Eucharistic sacrifice were in any way a natural sacrifice it would be simply impossible to avoid the conclusion that there
are two different sacrifices, and the query: Why two sacrifices? would
be most justifiable. . . . [I]f it be a sacrifice *in natura*, however it
be disguised, it is truly another sacrifice, and not the same sacrifice."[14]
There is no denying the force of this argument, and the underlying
difficulty has long been recognized. This aspect of the mystery
was first adverted to and clearly formulated by Saint John Chrysostom
in his Commentary on the Epistle to the Hebrews.

> In Christ the saving victim was offered once. Then what of ourselves? Do
> we not offer every day? Although we do offer daily, that is done for the
> recalling of his death, and the victim is one, not many. But how can that
> be—one and not many? Because Christ was immolated once. For this
> sacrifice is what corresponds to that sacrifice of his: the same reality, remain-
> ing always the same, is offered and so this is the same sacrifice. Otherwise,
> would you say that because the sacrifice is offered in many places, therefore
> there are many Christs? No, but there is one Christ in all those places,
> fully present here and fully present there. And just as what is offered in all
> places is one and the same body, so there is one and the same sacrifice.
> Christ offered a victim and we offer the selfsame now; but what we do is
> a recalling of his sacrifice. Nor is the sacrifice repeated because of its weakness
> (since it is what perfects mankind), but by reason of our own, because we
> sin daily.[15]

The problem is here clearly presented, and Clark tells us that
no other text from the Tradition was commented on more than this
one during the subsequent centuries.[16] Chrysostom saw the difficulty,
but, despite the difficulty, he was not tempted to deny the daily
sacrifice to make sense of it. "Do we not offer daily? Although we do
offer daily, " he wrote. And Saint Augustine saw the problem also, and
likewise saw no reason to deny the daily sacrifice when he wrote to
Boniface: "Was Christ not immolated once in Himself, and still in the
Sacrament, not only at every paschal solemnity but every day He is
immolated by the people, nor does he lie who responds to the question
that He is immolated?"[17] And none of the Catholic theologians who
followed after were tempted to deny the daily sacrifice either.

It was not until Luther and the Reformers that the theological
difficulty was turned into an objection to deny that the Eucharist is

a sacrifice in its own right. And Trent continued the line of Catholic Tradition by simply re-affirming the truth of the sacrifice in the Eucharist despite being unable to explain the apparent contradiction. And it is not that the precise problem of the unicity of Christ's Sacrifice of the Cross was not adverted to. It is true that the problem of the unicity of Christ's sacrifice was not taken seriously to begin with. It was only one of the different lines of attack put forward by Reformation theology, and the Catholics were so familiar with it from the Tradition that it didn't seem to pose any new or great difficulty. However, over the years of the Council, the point was taken up more seriously by Catholic theologians. Indeed, a group of highly competent Dominican theologians, who were influential bishops at the Council, argued the case very strongly at the Council itself, and still the conclusion was rejected. Now, given that the Council's teaching on this point seems to have passed somewhat into oblivion in Catholic theology, it is necessary to review what happened there in order to verify the accuracy of Rahner's confident assertion and to establish accurately exactly what the teaching of the Council was.

The Council of Trent on the Sacrifice of the Mass

In its treatment of the Mass, the Council of Trent was responding directly to Luther's denial of the sacrifice. This was a central element of Luther's platform, for he considered it "by far the most wicked abuse of all." He made the point vigorously in one of his three programmatic pamphlets of 1520. "The third captivity of this sacrament is by far the most wicked abuse of all, in consequence of which there is no opinion more generally held or more firmly believed in the church today than this, that the mass is a good work and a sacrifice."[18] And again: "Now there is yet a second stumbling block that must be removed, and this is much greater and the most dangerous of all. It is the common belief that the mass is a sacrifice which is offered to God."[19] It can hardly be doubted that Luther was denying that the Mass is a sacrifice in the plain and straightforward meaning, a "good work," something "offered to God," and that this is the faith of the Catholic Church, since "there is no opinion more generally held or more firmly believed in the church today than this." The issue was discussed at each session of the Council, and on each occasion one of the "errors" listed was to the effect that "the Eucharist is not a sacrifice . . . but only a commemoration of the Sacrifice of the Cross."[20]

At least one supporter of the purely sacramental sacrifice of the Eucharist has suggested that the appropriate response to Luther would have been along the lines of that theology. "The Protestant attack suggested a perfectly natural solution, in terms of the traditional definition of the mass as the sacramental representation of the passion. All that was necessary to say was that in the mass the sacrifice of the cross was made really present by means of this sacramental representation of the passion."[21] The Catholic theologians could have agreed with Luther that the Eucharist is not a natural sacrifice, but that neither is it a "mere" commemoration. It is a commemoration, indeed, but in what is taken to be the full biblical sense, making the reality remembered actual again in the present, and so can be legitimately recognized, on this basis, as a "true and proper" sacrifice.

The question is whether or not this response represents the faith of the Church. In fact, the Catholic theologians responded to Luther's denial with a strong affirmation of the sacrifice in the plain, straightforward sense that Luther was denying. As Hughes himself admits: "With a hundred variations they repeated that it *was* a sacrifice, and that it was utterly unheard of to question this truth."[22] And so indeed it was at the Council. At Bologna in August 1547, some of the theologians responded directly to Luther's assertion that the Eucharist is not a sacrifice but only a commemoration of the Sacrifice of the Cross. Six spoke directly to the point, and three managed to make the clear rebuttal that the Eucharist is not only a commemoration of the Sacrifice of the Cross, but a sacrifice that is celebrated in commemoration of the Sacrifice of the Cross. One affirms: "that the offering in the Mass is a commemoration of the Sacrifice of the Cross, but not only a commemoration, but also a sacrifice, and this sacrifice is a memorial of the Sacrifice of the Cross."[23] At Trent in 1551, three theologians speak to this point on this occasion, and this time only one, the famous Melchior Cano, managed to state explicitly that "if we do not offer a sacrifice, we do not represent the Sacrifice of Christ offered on the Cross."[24]

That a sacrifice in the plain meaning of the word was being affirmed is made clear by the arguments brought forward in support of the proposition. It was surely a handicap in rebutting Luther's denial that the theologians had no clear idea what a sacrifice is and that they had no tradition of dealing with this question to refer to. They did what Catholic theology had been doing for centuries and based themselves on the teaching of the Fathers of the Church in the matter. The discussions ranged over many areas, but a perusal of the minutes makes clear that two particular lines of patristic teaching predominate in the final decree, and we will deal with them in turn.

The Eucharist as a Natural Sacrifice

The first stream of tradition is precisely to the effect that the Eucharist is a natural sacrifice continuous with the sacrifices of the Old Testament. This teaching was first clearly formulated by Saint Irenaeus and subsequently became standard. Saint Irenaeus deals with the issue of sacrifice in chapters 17 and 18 of Book 4 of the *Adversus Haereses*. He begins by discussing the prophetic critique of sacrifice in the Old Testament, introducing it as follows: "The prophets indicate abundantly that it was not because He had need of their service that God prescribed the observances contained in the Law; and the Lord, in His turn, taught openly that God demands an offering for the sake of man who is offering."[25] After a thorough review of the prophetic teaching, making it clear that the prophets were not attacking the institution of sacrifice, but sacrifice that is not accompanied by a sincere religious spirit, he repeats again our Lord's attitude to sacrifice. "To His disciples also, He counselled the offering to God of the first fruits of His creatures."[26] He elaborates the point shortly after. "Therefore, the offering of the Church, which the Lord taught should be offered in the whole world, is to be reckoned a pure sacrifice before God and acceptable to Him, not because He has need of our sacrifice, but that the one who offers is glorified in what he offers if his gift is accepted."[27] He makes his point most clearly in a further text which was to become a classic reference. "And the class of offerings has not been abrogated; for there were offerings there, and there are offerings here. Sacrifices there were in the People; sacrifices there are, too, in the Church: but the species alone has been changed, inasmuch as the offering is now made, not by slaves but by freemen."[28]

Saint Irenaeus is clearly affirming that the Christian sacrifice is to be understood as standing in continuity with the Old Testament sacrifices and uses the standard sacrificial terminology to express himself. It is a stronger statement of this opinion than any that went before, and interpreters have sought reasons to explain Irenaeus's heavy emphasis on this aspect. The explanation is usually found in the fact that Saint Irenaeus was rebutting the over-spiritualized doctrine of the Gnostics, and that he exaggerated in the opposite direction. This would seem to be a doubtful explanation. To suggest that Saint Irenaeus distorted the faith of the Church to make a debating point is hardly to do justice to his reputation as a Father of the Church. However, our immediate interest here is not in seeking an interpretation of the reason why Saint Irenaeus taught as he did, but in the fact of his teaching and the use made of this line of patristic interpretation at the Council of Trent, where it was officially sanctioned.

The discussion of the Decree on the Sacrifice of the Mass began at Bologna in 1547, and at the first meeting of the theologians discussing the "errors," this point about the natural sacrifice was made by five of the theologians who spoke. All we have are short summaries of their speeches, but even in the form of the minutes it is clear what was being said. There is sacrifice according to the natural law, according to the Law in the Old Testament, and there must be sacrifice now in the Christian dispensation, which is the perfection of all that went before.[29] These men are simply repeating Saint Irenaeus and the other Fathers of the Church who made this same point.

Nothing further was done at that time, and when the issue came up for discussion the second time, in Trent in December 1551, the formulation of this particular "error" had been enlarged to include the denial that the Eucharist is a "true and proper" sacrifice, and a draft of canons was produced, the first of which anathematized these denials. In the discussion of the theologians, this issue was not greatly in evidence, since by this time attention was focused elsewhere, as we shall see. However, lack of mention did not at all imply any less emphasis on the doctrine. In January 1552, a committee set about drafting a new version of the decree. In the accompanying Doctrinal Statement on the Mass, the point which had been made at Bologna in 1547 was included. It was affirmed that "the abolition of the sacrifices of the Old Testament [did not] deprive [Christians] of the whole reality of

sacrifice [*sacrificandi rationem*], but rather a new and clearly divine
sacrifice was bequeathed to the Christian priests."[30] And later the
statement asserts: "Nor would it be fitting, clearly, if the New Law, which
is perfect in every way, were to lack any external and visible sacrifice."[31]
On this occasion the sacrament of Orders was being discussed at
the same time, and the following day the same committee produced
a draft of a set of canons on the sacrament of Orders that would
anathematize anyone who would deny that "in the New Testament there
is a visible and external priesthood."[32] This same teaching was included
in the Doctrinal Statement on the Sacrament of Orders, where it is
affirmed that "in the Church of God there is an external sacrifice, and
therefore a visible and external priesthood."[33] These are strong
affirmations of a "visible and external priesthood" offering an "external
and visible sacrifice" in continuity with the "reality of sacrifice" of the
Old Testament. If this draft had been promulgated as it stands, there
would hardly have been any doubt as to the "plain and obvious"
meaning of the teaching of the Council, but the situation was to change
quite considerably before the final decree was produced in 1562. The
controversy arose concerning the second major line of patristic interpretation, and this first affirmation of the natural sacrifice was only
very lightly treated after 1551. The little that further needs to be said
about it will be placed in its temporal sequence when we discuss the
major debate of 1562.

According to the Order of Melchizedek

A second line of patristic teaching which came to dominate the
conciliar debate is one which sees in the Last Supper and the Eucharist
the fulfilment of the prophecy in Psalm 110:4: "You are a priest forever
according to the order of Melchizedek."[34] The Fathers understood
this according to a simple schema. Melchizedek offered sacrifice
in bread and wine, and so, in fulfilment of the figure, Christ our Lord
offered sacrifice in bread and wine and commanded that the same be
done in his memory. This came to be a hotly debated issue at the
Council, and the theologians defending this interpretation as the faith
of the Church drew up lists of patristic texts in its favor,[35] so a short
presentation of the patristic doctrine is again in order.

The first evidence of this relating of the Melchizedek figure to the Last Supper and the Eucharist is to be found in Clement of Alexandria, and all he does is mention it. It was taken up and maintained in both the East and the West, as the list of texts compiled makes clear. However, of these texts, only two develop the doctrine at any length, and of those two by far the fuller is Saint Cyprian's Letter 63 to Caecilium,[36] and it is quite obvious from a perusal of the minutes of Trent that this letter was the foundation of what the theologians and the bishops were all saying. It relates directly to the issue under discussion, the sacrificial character of the Eucharist on the level of the liturgy itself. What prompted Saint Cyprian to write to his fellow Bishop Caecilium was the fact that in some places Christians had begun celebrating the Eucharist using only water instead of wine mixed with water, and Cyprian wrote to condemn this practice.

He opens the letter by stating the problem as he sees it, mentioning that "some either from ignorance or simplicity in blessing the Lord's chalice and ministering to the people do not do what Jesus Christ our Lord and God, author and teacher of this sacrifice did and taught. . . ."[37] He then lays down the principle to be applied. "You know we have been warned that in offering the Lord's chalice we must follow tradition and we should do nothing different from that which the Lord first did for us, that the chalice which is offered in His memory should be offered mixed with wine."[38] Then he applies the figure of Melchizedek:

> Likewise, in the priest Melchizedek, we see the sacrament of the sacrifice of the Lord prefigured. . . . This order, indeed, is the one coming from that sacrifice and thence descending because Melchizedek was a priest of the most high God, because he offered bread, because he blessed Abraham. For who is more a priest of the most high God than our Lord Jesus Christ, who offered sacrifice to God the Father and offered the very same thing which Melchizedek had offered, bread and wine, that is, actually, His Body and Blood. . . . the image of the sacrifice goes before, appointed actually in bread and wine. Accomplishing and fulfilling this action, the Lord offered bread and a chalice mixed with wine. . . . [39]

For the rest of the letter he continues emphasizing and repeating these same points, that Christ offered bread and wine, and that we must do what he did. One example will suffice. "For if in the sacrifice which

Christ offered, only Christ is to be followed, likewise we must obey and do what Christ did and what he commanded to be done. . . ."[40] With this background in mind, we can now examine what happened at the Council.

This point was raised by the theologians during the first meeting at Bologna in 1547. Five of them mentioned it, and the influence of Saint Cyprian is plain to be seen. One of them said: "The sacrifice of Melchizedek was the type and figure of the sacrifice of the Eucharist. Just as Melchizedek offered bread and wine, so the priest offers bread and wine, so that it will be transubstantiated into the Body of Christ."[41] Another formulated it as follows: "Moreover, if Christ sacrificed to the Father in bread and wine and said 'Do this in memory of me,' therefore the priest does the same in the Mass."[42] In 1551, when the Council reconvened at Trent, this point came more to the fore, and now the focus was on the sacrificial quality of the Last Supper itself. The issue must have arisen in controversy in the meantime, because even before the discussion of the sacrifice of the Mass began, many of the theologians had presented lists of errors for discussion, and among the errors listed by almost all of them was the denial of this teaching that Christ had offered a sacrifice at the Last Supper.[43] Although no mention of the point appeared on the official list of errors proposed for discussion, the interventions were more frequent than at Bologna and reported at greater length. The basic affirmations are the same as before, the only new point being the introduction of the phrase "under the appearances of bread and wine." "And since Christ is a priest according to the order of Melchizedek, it is necessary that he sacrificed according to the order of Melchizedek, in bread and wine. Christ only did that at the Last Supper, therefore Christ at the Last Supper offered His body under these appearances (*sub illis speciebus*)."[44]

Until this point no controversy had arisen in these discussions. This situation changed dramatically, however, when the Council Fathers came to discuss the draft of the chapters and canons on Orders and on the Mass in January 1552, when there began a heated debate which would not end until the Council closed ten years later. A group of Dominican bishops, all of whom had studied at the University of Salamanca, began what seems to have been a concerted effort to overturn the consensus on this issue. A study of their different interventions at the Council makes it clear that their opinion was substantially the same as that which has now come to be widely accepted in Catholic theology. They did not accept the "true and proper," "visible and external" sacrifice of the Mass, though this was not explicitly the point they opposed. They focused their attack on the Melchizedek prophecy and the Last Supper sacrifice, with the teaching on the sacrifice of the Mass understood to be at stake by implication.

The first of them to speak was Pedro Guerrero, Archbishop of Granada, who would be a central figure in the drama right to the end. He objected to the use of the Melchizedek prophecy on the grounds that it is doubtful if Melchizedek offered sacrifice at all in Genesis 14:18,[45] and he was followed in this by another Salamanca Dominican, Tomás Campegi, Bishop of Feltri,[46] who added his opinion that Hebrews 7:1ff. does not refer to Melchizedek's sacrifice but to his lack of genealogy, thus referring to the eternity of Christ's priesthood.[47] Then came the intervention that shocked the Council and remained the focus of all attention in this debate until it concluded in 1562.[48] It was another of the Salamanca Dominicans, Cornelio Musso, Bishop of Bitonto, who said he disapproved "that it is said that Christ offered himself at the Last Supper, because then he would have died in vain, because that [sacrifice] would have sufficed to reconcile us with God."[49]

In this first denial of the sacrifice at the Last Supper, the Bishop of Bitonto gave the fundamental reason that was to cause the difficulty, that a sacrifice at the Last Supper is incompatible with the unicity of the Sacrifice of the Cross, the same objection, notice, that Luther had already used and that Vonier would subsequently use to deny the natural sacrifice. These denials of the sacrifice of Melchizedek and the sacrifice of the Last Supper were almost unanimously rejected by the other bishops. Five of the bishops reaffirmed the Melchizedek prophecy,[50] and many more rejected the denial of the Last Supper sacrifice.[51] One after another, they affirmed that Christ offered a sacrifice at the Last Supper, according to the order of Melchizedek, with only one, yet another Dominican from Salamanca, supporting Musso.[52]

A revised version of the Doctrinal Statement was presented on January 20, 1552. We have already pointed out that it contained a strong statement of the natural sacrifice, and it also contained a strong statement of this doctrine of the Last Supper sacrifice, presenting it as the primary reason in favor of the sacrifice of the Mass.

That the Mass is a true and proper sacrifice is shown first of all by the oath of God the Father: "You are a priest forever, according to the order of Melchizedek" (Ps. 109:4). Christ our Lord exercised this priesthood, when he offered Himself to His Father at the Last Supper under the sensible appearances of bread and wine, and He will not cease to offer through priests who exercise His ministry, just as Melchizedek himself offered bread and wine in sacrifice to God.[53]

It was not possible to conclude the work on these documents at this session of the Council, and so it was not until ten years later that the debate was resumed.

The Debate of 1562

When the Council reconvened at Trent in 1562, the situation was completely transformed. This time one of the presidents of the Council, Geronimo Seripando, was firmly against the idea of the Last Supper as a sacrifice and the whole related emphasis on the visible sacrifice of the Mass, and that meant that the whole discussion had to start again from the beginning. A new list of "errors" was drawn up and a new draft of chapters and canons.[54] One of the members of the commission established to produce a new draft of the decree was none other than Pedro Guerrero, Archbishop of Granada, who had argued against the Last Supper sacrifice in 1551. He was opposed in the commission by Antonio Panthusa, Bishop of Lettere, but since Seripando, as one of the presidents of the Council and also opposed to the doctrine, was the referee in the dispute, the result was to be expected. When the document was produced, the doctrine of the sacrifice of the Last Supper, together with the strong statements on the "true and proper" sacrifice of the draft of 1551, had been completely set aside, and so the scene was set for a vigorous debate when the document came for examination in the General Congregations.[55]

The section of the chapter that spoke of the Last Supper read as follows:

And to speak first of the institution of this sacrifice, it is to be held that Christ our Lord instituted it when at the Last Supper, changing bread and wine into His Body and Blood, He offered Himself under the symbols of these things to the Apostles to be eaten and offered and commanded them saying: "Do this in memory of me." The Church has always understood these words as a command to priests to offer this sacrifice in memory of Christ.[56]

It is to be noted that there is no mention of the Last Supper as a sacrifice, no mention of Melchizedek. Christ "offered Himself under the symbols of these things to the Apostles," not to God. This formulation is closer to Luther than to the text produced eleven years before. The new draft was first discussed by the theologians on July 19, 1562. The withdrawal of the draft of 1551, with its strong affirmation of the natural sacrifice, probably explains why five of those who spoke are recorded as making the same point that had been made at Bologna in 1547 that the Christian sacrifice is according to human nature and in continuity with the sacrifices of the Old Testament.[57] There was also almost complete unanimity among them that the Melchizedek prophecy and the doctrine of the sacrifice at the Last Supper should be restored to the decree, with only one dissenting voice, that of another Dominican from Salamanca.

This near unanimity among the theologians against this draft had no impact on the situation, and in the draft of chapters and canons submitted to the Council Fathers on August 6, 1562, there was still no mention of the Last Supper sacrifice. The section dealing with the point about the Mass as a "true and proper" sacrifice remains very much watered down and contains none of the language of the "external and visible" sacrifice from the draft of 1551.[58] This second point, however, was not addressed at all in the General Congregation, since all the attention was focused on the Last Supper sacrifice. When the Council Fathers began the discussion of the decree on August 11, 1562, the first to speak was one of the presidents of the Council, Cardinal Madras. He set the agenda of the whole debate when he pronounced his opinion that the doctrinal statement should speak of the sacrifice "which Christ offered at the Last Supper," and that "Do this in memory of me" should be explained to mean that "Christ offered at the Last Supper, and commanded to be done what He himself had done when he offered according to the order of Melchizedek at the Last Supper."[59] This was effectively the only issue of substance addressed throughout the debate. Every one of the 137 Fathers who spoke expressed an opinion one way or the other, and a statistical analysis was done by Alonso in his book. Five of the Fathers explicitly

denied the sacrifice, 91 explicitly affirmed it, 33 accepted it with certain reservations, and of 14 it is hard to say what exactly their position
was. Four Fathers expressed themselves indifferent on the question,
and about the other nine it is not clear whether they spoke at all.[60] The
opponents of the doctrine were the same five Dominicans from
Salamanca, and the basic argument was the same. Christ cannot have
offered sacrifice at the Last Supper because there is only one sacrifice,
the Sacrifice of the Cross. Many of the bishops made clear that they
simply did not know where the truth lay. Various difficulties were put
forward; different suggestions made. The debate is a marvelous mine
of arguments on one side and the other, but this is not the moment to
enter into such a discussion or to attempt to resolve the difficulties
with the doctrine, which are very real. Our interest is in knowing what
the doctrine is, what the Council finally decided on the issue.

The point at issue was clear to all. Did Christ offer sacrifice at
the Last Supper according to the order of Melchizedek, in other
words, in bread and wine? And did he command the apostles to do
what he had done, so that the Eucharist is likewise a sacrifice under
the appearances of bread and wine? This doctrine is in response to
Luther's denial of the sacrifice of the Mass, and the response is a direct
contradiction of his denial. The precise point debated was about the
Last Supper sacrifice, but the related positions were all understood.
The debate ended on August 27 and the decree was rewritten to meet
the desire of the majority. The point about the natural sacrifice, so
much emphasised in the draft of 1551, was restored in a single clause
asserting that Christ instituted the Eucharist "in order to leave to his
beloved Spouse the Church a visible sacrifice (as human nature
demands) . . . " (DS 1740/ND 1546), corresponding to the first
canon, which states: "If anyone says that in the Mass a true and proper
sacrifice is not offered to God . . . *anathema sit*" (DS 1751/ND
1555). Even though the reference to this point is so small as to appear
almost negligible, it is clear that the doctrine so fully formulated in the
draft of 1551 was being affirmed by the Council. Any doubt that
might remain on this point regarding the visible, natural sacrifice can
be overcome by reference to the Decree on the Sacrament of Orders
which was promulgated in the subsequent 23rd Session. There the
Council taught on the sacrament of Orders: "Sacrifice and priesthood
are by the ordinance of God so united that both have existed under

every law. Since, therefore, in the New Testament the Catholic Church has received from the institution of Christ the holy, visible sacrifice of the Eucharist, it must also be acknowledged that there exists in the Church a new, visible and external priesthood into which the old one was changed" (DS 1764/ND 1707). And Canon 1 corresponding reads: "If anyone says that there is in the New Testament no visible and external priesthood . . . *anathema sit*" (DS 1771/ND 1714). In regard to the Last Supper sacrifice, Cardinal Madruzzo's suggestion was implemented and the doctrine asserts that "declaring himself constituted 'a priest forever according to the order of Melchizedek' (Ps 109:4), [Christ] offered his body and blood under the species of bread and wine to God the Father, and under the same signs gave them to partake of to the disciples (whom he established as priests of the New Testament), and ordered them and their successors in the priesthood to offer, saying: 'Do this in memory of me,' etc. (Lk 22:19; 1 Cor 11:24) as the Catholic Church has always understood and taught" (DS 1740/ND 1546). And the corresponding second canon reads: "If anyone says that by the words 'Do this in memory of me' (Lk 22:19; 1 Cor 11:24) Christ did not establish the apostles as priests or that he did not order that they should offer his body and blood, *anathema sit*" (DS 1752/ND 1556).

In the light of what we have seen, it can hardly be doubted what the teaching of the Council is. The doctrine that the Eucharist is a visible, a true and proper sacrifice, traditional for centuries and taken for granted by the vast majority of those involved, was clearly affirmed. That much is admitted even by those who do not accept the teaching. We saw earlier that John Jay Hughes suggested that Trent should have taught otherwise, implicitly accepting the fact of the clear teaching that was given. Edward J. Kilmartin, too, who rejects the opinion, concedes that it was taught by Trent. "The Council of Trent . . . teaches that through the offering of the body and blood of Christ under the forms of bread and wine, the Eucharist is a visible sacrifice which, in itself, has a sacrificial character. . . . In other words, the commemorative actual presence of the sacrifice of the cross is not identified as the ground of the sacrificial character of the Mass. Rather, it is the sacrificial character of the Mass that grounds why it can represent the sacrifice of the cross."[61] What is new in the Tridentine teaching is the affirmation of the sacrificial quality of the Last Supper itself. This point was implicit in the Cyprianic reasoning, that what Christ did we also must do, but it had never before been explicitly formulated. The point was not spelled out in a clear definition, but it was taught, and the only remaining question is as to the status of this teaching. Did the Council make a binding judgment on this matter? Some say not. Consider, for example, Raymond Moloney.

> One of the hotly debated points in this chapter was whether the Last Supper was to be regarded as a sacrifice. The affirmative view seemed to many to take from the propitiatory function of the Cross. The negative view seemed to create a dichotomy between the Last Supper and the sacrifice of the Mass. From the perspective of present-day theology we can interpret this dispute as a conflict between notions of natural sacrifice and sacramental sacrifice, which were not fully worked out at that time. Fortunately the Council did not decide the issue in a fundamental way. They were content to teach in the first chapter of the decree that in the Last Supper Christ offered himself, but they left open how this was related to the other aspects of Christ's sacrifice.[62]

One has to admit that on the basis of the text of the final decree taken by itself, the issue is not clear. However, as a help to the formation of a judgment on the correct answer to this question, there are a few significant points of information available. At the stage of the final drafting of the decree, the effort was made to avoid issuing a definitive judgement on this point. Cardinal Seripando and those against the Last Supper sacrifice insisted that the phrase "which is the opinion of the Fathers" (*ut est patrum sententia*) be added to the sentence affirming the sacrifice, and it was contained in the draft presented on September 5. However, on September 6 the Council was informed that this phrase was to be removed, by order of the papal legates.[63] During the discussion begun on September 7, the vast majority simply agreed: *Placet.* Of those few opposed, Guerrero was the only one opposed to the affirmation of the Last Supper sacrifice in any sense. "He warned the Fathers, that before they establish a dogma of faith, they should give the matter diligent and mature consideration beforehand."[64] He caused great annoyance by staying away from the public session on September 17, and when he was prevailed upon to return, he entered a statement into the record which stated, among other things, that: "he did not agree to its being defined, that Christ offered Himself at the Last Supper, since the holy doctors assert that *He only did this once.*"[65]

It is clear that the Archbishop of Granada considered that the Council was proposing a doctrine as of faith in this matter. And he was not alone. Another bishop, writing to Cardinal Morone, relates his amazement that without having much time for study the bishops were able to settle this question so quickly. He mentions the matter of the phrase "as many Fathers have said" and the fact that the papal legates had removed the qualification, and concludes: "And so we are making an article of faith without the testimony of Scripture and without apostolic tradition, and of something one has never heard spoken of in the schools."[66] One last witness in this line is worth adverting to. On September 16, on the eve of the public session to proclaim the decree, Cardinal Seripando himself presented a minute to his fellow papal legates requesting a solemn declaration that he, Cardinal Seripando, disapproved of the decree. The first papal legate, Cardinal Hercules Gonzaga, signed the declaration, the first sentence of which says:

> We, Hercules etc., do solemnly affirm that, Geronimo Cardinal Seripando, in the private meetings of the Papal Legates, never wished to consent that in the decree on the Sacrifice of the Mass, anything should be written as certain, indubitable, and of faith regarding the oblation or immolation or sacrifice of Christ our Lord in the Last Supper, and he asserted that he was moved to this view by reasons which he presented to us in writing.[67]

These are just a few witnesses, but they include important figures in the Council. The two men most opposed to the declaration, Archbishop Guerrero and Cardinal Seripando, were both convinced that a binding judgment was being made. It stands to reason also that the papal legates did not dispute Seripando's assessment of what was being done, since they could easily have disabused him, and it was precisely they who removed the qualifying clause which Guerrero and Seripando held dear. Weighing all the evidence, one would find it hard to fault the judgement on this issue of a recent commentator. "The sacrificial character of the Last Supper was not formally defined; however, despite the strong objections made and the difficulties that became clear during the debate, it was restored to the doctrinal section of the Decree and, on September 17th, solemnly proclaimed as the teaching of the Council and, therefore, of the Church."[68]

This teaching that the Last Supper was a sacrifice will be of interest in our further discussion in due course. However, it is clear that this teaching on the Last Supper sacrifice is not being affirmed in isolation, as a question on its own. It represents the keystone of an interlocking set of doctrines that constitutes the Council's reply to Luther's denial of the visible sacrifice of the Eucharist from which the discussion began. This is the point of immediate interest to us here, and there can be no doubt that Rahner's short summary of the "plain and obvious" teaching of the Church in this matter is completely accurate. We set out to re-establish the traditional position that the Eucharist is a sacrifice in its own right, and that has been done. We are ready, then, to proceed to the task we have set ourselves of presenting an alternative concept of sacrifice which can make sense of that affirmation. Before leaving this preliminary discussion, it must be noted that the difficulty raised by Luther, the Salamanca Dominicans, and Vonier as to how the sacrifice in the Eucharist does not conflict with the doctrine of the unicity of the Sacrifice of the Cross has not yet been resolved. There are pointers towards a solution to be found in the Tridentine discussions, but it seems wiser to leave a consideration of this point until later, when the sacrificial quality of the Eucharist has been more clearly established.

---

1. "In primis autem est Eucharistia sacrificium." *Dominicae Coenae* (1980), II 9, AAS 72 (1980), 130.

2. Hans Küng, *On Being a Christian* (London: SCM, 1977), 425.

3. Raymond Moloney, *The Eucharist* (London: Geoffrey Chapman, 1995), 212.

4. Edward J. Kilmartin, sj, *The Eucharist in the West* (Collegeville, Minnesota: The Liturgical Press, 1998), xxiv.

5. M. Lepin, *L'Idée du sacrifice de la Messe d'après les théologiens* (Paris: Gabriel Beauchesne, 1926), 215–220.

6. Francis Clark, sj, *Eucharistic Sacrifice and the Reformation* (Oxford: Blackwell, 1967), 442.

7. Clark, *Eucharistic Sacrifice and the Reformation*, 442–443.

8. Karl Rahner and Angelus Häussling, *The Celebration of the Eucharist* (London/New York: Burns & Oates/Herder and Herder, 1968), 13.

9. Dom Anscar Vonier, osb, *A Key to the Doctrine of the Eucharist* (London: Burns, Oates & Washbourne, 1925), 87.

10. Kilmartin, *The Eucharist in the West*, 184.

11. Rahner and Häussling, *The Celebration of the Eucharist*, 13–14.

12. Ibid., 18.

13. Ibid., 13.

14. Vonier, *A Key to the Doctrine of the Eucharist*, 135.

15. Clark, *Eucharistic Sacrifice and the Reformation*. This is Peter Lombard's version from IV *Sent.*, d. 12, c. 5, translated and quoted by Clark on page 75.

16. Clark, *Eucharistic Sacrifice and the Reformation*, 75.

17. Augustine, *Ep. 98 Bonifatio episcopo*, § 9; CSEL 34, 2, 530, 21–531, 3; PL 33, 363.

18. Martin Luther, "The Babylonian Captivity of the Church" (1520), in Abdel Ross Wentz, editor and Helmut Lehmann, general editor, *Luther's Works* Volume 36 (Philadelphia: Fortress Press, 1959), 11–126, at 35.

19. Ibid., 51.

20. CT VI, 322.1–3.

21. John Jay Hughes, *Stewards of the Lord* (London and Sydney: Sheed and Ward, 1970), 104.

22. Hughes, *Stewards of the Lord*, 112.

23. CT VI, 350.27–30.

24. CT VII, I, 389.8–10.

25. *Adv. Haer.* IV, 17, 1; SC 100, 574–575.

26. *Adv. Haer.* IV, 17, 5; SC 100, 590–591.

27. *Adv. Haer.* IV, 18, 1; SC 100, 595–597.

28. *Adv. Haer.* IV, 18, 2; SC 100, 598–599.

29. CT VI, 325.18–19; 327.9–10; 334.16–18; 337.1–2; 345.41–346.1.

30. CT VII, I, 475.18–19.

31. CT VII, I, 478.8–9.

32. CT VII, I, 461.1.

33. CT VII, I, 485.23–24.

34. On this see Manuel Alonso, sj, *El Sacrificio Eucarístico de la última cena del Señor según el Concilio Tridentino* (Madrid, 1929).

35. From the lists minuted, the texts I could verify were the following: Clement of Alexandria; *Stromata* IV, xxv. (PG 8, 1369/1370B.); Cyprian,

Epist. 63 ad Caecilium (PL 4, 376A; CSEL III, II, 703ff.; CCL, III C, 389ff.); Ambrose; *De Abraham,* I 3, 16 (PL 14 427A; CSEL XXXII, I, 514, 4 ss.); *De sacramentis* IV 3 (PL 16, 438, CSEL LXXIII 50, 16–17.); Augustine, *De civitate Dei* XVI 22 (PL 41, 500; CSEL, XL, II, 164, 3 ss.); *ad Innocentium I epist.* 177 (olim 95), c. 12 (CSEL XLIV 681, 5s.; *De doctrina Christ.* IV 21, 45 (CCL XXXII 152, 29–33, quoting Cyprian 703, 1–5.); Jerome, *ad Marcellum epist.* 46, 2 (CSEL LIV 331, 14–17); John Chrysostom, *Hom. de Melchisedeco* (PG LVI 261ff.); Chrysostom, *In Genesim homil.* 35, 3 (PG LIII 328); Theophylact, *Expositio in epist. ad Hebr.* 5:6 (PG CXXV 241D [Migne has C twice on this page].); John Damascene, *De fide orthodoxa* IV 13 (PG 94, 1149C).

36. The other is Chrysostom's homily on Melchizedek.

37. CCL, III C, 389.7ss.

38. Ibid., 391.22ss.

39. Ibid., 392.40ss. (Alternative references: Cyprian, *Epist. 63 ad Caecilium* (PL 4, 376A; CSEL III, II, 703, 1ss.). English trans., *The Fathers of the Church* (Washington: The Catholic University of America Press, 1964), 4.

40. Ibid., 409.254 ss.

41. CT VI, 350.17–19.

42. CT VI, 361.19–20.

43. Some examples in CT VII, II, 350, 21–24; 363, 1–3; 366, 18–19.

44. CT VII, I, 411.9–13.

45. CT VII, I, 445.22–23.

46. CT VII, I, 446.7–8.

47. CT VII, I, 446.9–12.

48. Melchior Cano was later to comment that this assertion came as a complete surprise to all the bishops and theologians at the Council (*a patribus et theologis universis explosum*). De Locis XII, 12.

49. CT VII, I, 449.27–28.

50. CT VII, I, 446.26–27; 447.30–32; 448.22; 452.31–33; 454.28–30.

51. CT VII, II, 450.8–10; 450.31–32; 451.14–23; 451.33–34; 453.3–4; 453.13–25; 454.7–11; 455.9–18; 456.2; 456.12–15; 457.9–15; 457.24–26; 458.29–30; 459.1.

52. CT VII, I, 459.9–18.

53. CT VII, I, 475.20–24.

54. Alonso, 122.

55. Ibid., 131.

56. CT VIII, 751.15–21.

57. CT VIII, 727.5–6, 26–29; 728.5–11; 740.21–25; 744.32–39.

58. CT VIII, 751.10–15.

59. CT VIII, 755.10–13.

60. Alonso, *El Sacrificio Eucarístico*, 192.

61. Kilmartin, *The Eucharist in the West*, 176f.

62. Moloney, *The Eucharist*, 169f.

63. CT VIII, 879.1–3.

64. "admonuit Patres, ut antequam dogma fidei constituant, omnia prius diligenter et mature considerare velint." CT VIII, 954.23–24.

65. "Non item placet definiri, Christum in coena se obtulisse, cum sancti doctores asseverent *illum semel hoc fecisse*." CT VIII, 964.1–2.

66. "Mutinensis: Et così facciamo un articolo di fede senza testimonio della Scrittura et senza traditione apostolica, et d'una cosa, della quale mai si sentì parlare nelle schole." CT VIII, 915, fn. 2.

67. Alonso, *El Sacrificio Eucarístico*, 227–228.

68. Erwin Iserloh, "Das tridentinische Messopferdekret in seinen Beziehungen zu der Kontroverstheologie der Zeit," in *Il concilio di Trento e la riforma tridentina: Atti del convegno storico internazionale, Trento–2–6 Settembre, 1963*, Volume II (Herder, 1965), 401–439, at p. 437. Also in *Concilium Tridentinum* (hrsg. von R. Bäumer), (Darmstadt, 1979), 341–381, at p. 379.

Chapter 2

Two Old Testament Models of Sacrifice

Before presenting the model of sacrifice which it will be suggested corresponds to the Eucharist, it will be useful to outline the notion currently taken for granted in Christian theology, for there is a notion of sacrifice at work even when it is not explicitly adverted to. As Karl Rahner pointed out, the suggestion that theology has no need of a concept of sacrifice is epistemologically untenable. If a word is used in intelligent discourse, it has a meaning. The meaning may not be explicitly formulated, but a meaning there must be. And it is so in this case, for the fact of the matter is that there has been a dominant notion of sacrifice operative in Western theology for a thousand years or more. During all this time, the Cross of Christ has been the one universally accepted sacrifice with which people were familiar, and the notion of sacrifice was drawn from a consideration of the Cross as the primary analogate of sacrifice. The Cross is understood as Christ's offering of himself to the Father, and his offering is understood to be made effective by his death. He is the Priest and the Victim of the sacrifice and the act of sacrifice is understood to be this single all-embracing act, on the Cross, which effectively begins and ends the sacrifice. All that precedes and follows is understood to be ancillary to the one central act of sacrifice which is Christ's death on the Cross. According to F.C.N. Hicks: "The 'man in the street,' and many who are more familiar with theology than he, would still, if they were asked to describe a sacrifice, suggest an altar, with a living victim bound upon it, and a priest standing over it with a knife in his uplifted hand. Translated into the language of Christian sacrifice, that is the conception of Christ offering Himself upon the Altar of the Cross, of sacrifice as equivalent to, and completed in, death."[1]

Within this overall structure many variations are possible. One can stress the change which must take place in the victim, its destruction or death, or one can stress the self-sacrificial will of the priest offering the sacrifice, and different combinations have been proposed. However, all are united in the fundamental structure that there is the Priest offering himself as the Victim in the one all-embracing act that took place on Calvary. When one comes, then, to apply this notion to the Eucharist, one looks to find the representation of Calvary in the liturgy. This effort began during the medieval period.[2] The medieval liturgical commentators sought in the actions of the Mass symbols of the Passion of Christ. The Canon was taken as symbolic of the whole set of events of Holy Week, beginning from the entry into Jerusalem. The priest holding his arms extended could recall the arms of Christ extended on the Cross. When the priest bows, he recalls Christ bowing his head in death. Every action of the priest with the sacred host can be read as symbolic: taking it, holding it, raising it, lowering it, breaking it, and so on. For instance, the elevation of the host and the chalice after the Consecration could symbolize the raising of Christ on the Cross and the shedding of his blood for our salvation. The Fraction obviously lends itself to a symbolic interpretation, and could easily refer to the breaking of the body of Christ in death. More recently, this symbolic interpretation of the various gestures of the priest has been abandoned, and the representation of Calvary is understood to be found in the Eucharistic Prayer itself, with the separation of the body and blood of Christ in the consecration of the bread and wine seen as being of central significance. Typical of this would be the formulation of Pope Pius XII in *Mediator Dei:* "The unbloody immolation at the words of consecration, when Christ is made present upon the altar in the state of victim, is performed by the priest . . . [and] it is because the priest places the divine victim upon the altar that he offers it to God the Father as an oblation for the glory of the Blessed Trinity and for the good of the whole Church."[3] On this approach, there is one single act of sacrifice, when the priest offers the body and blood of Christ in the Eucharistic Prayer, and what precedes in the Offertory and what follows in Communion are understood as related to the sacrifice but ancillary to it.

This model of sacrifice is fundamentally the structure of one of the Old Testament sacrifices, the holocaust, or burnt offering. It is the first model of sacrifice to be found in the Bible, and the only one during the patriarchal period. The three notable examples are the sacrifice of Noah (Genesis 8:20), Abraham's sacrifice of Isaac (Genesis 22:2), and the sacrifice of Elijah on Mount Carmel (1 Kings 18:38). In the holocaust, an animal is killed and burned before God as an act of humble submission and thanksgiving, and it serves as the basic model of sacrifice in current Western theology, as it has done for many centuries. It is the sacrifice that Saint Paul had in mind in Ephesians 5:2 when he wrote: "Christ loved us and handed Himself over as an offering and sacrifice to God in the odour of sweetness." It has the advantage of accounting well for the centrality of our Lord's saving death, where what is pleasing to God the Father is the total gift of himself made by His Son, and there is no question, therefore, that this notion of sacrifice goes to the heart of the matter. It does not, however, cover every aspect. It does not account for every dimension of the Sacrifice of the Cross itself, as we shall see in due course, but its most immediate disadvantage, from the point of view of the current discussion, is that it has not permitted a satisfactory explanation of the sacrificial nature of the Eucharist. After centuries of careful reflection based on this model of sacrifice, all the sacrificial significance of the Eucharist is condensed into the Eucharistic Prayer, and the other two important parts of the liturgy, the Offertory and Communion, are not seen as being essential elements of the sacrificial action at all.

The proposal to be made here is that a different starting point is needed, in a more comprehensive notion of sacrifice. The full sacrificial experience of Israel should be brought into play: the Passover, the covenant sacrifice of Sinai, and the complex and beautiful liturgy of the Temple described in Leviticus chapters 1 to 7, namely, holocausts, communion sacrifices, and sin offerings, the most important of which is the national rite of purification on the Day of Atonement. Our Lord said that he came not to abolish the Law and the Prophets but to fulfill them (Matthew 5:17). This plan of his must apply also to the culminating point of Old Testament religion, its worship. The pious Jew lived his religious life around the experience of sacrifice the way we live our Christian lives around the Eucharist, and that loving experience of sacrifice must be recovered and appreciated before an appropriate understanding of sacrifice can be formulated. It will be argued that the notion currently operative in theology, while being deep and profound, is too narrow in its scope, and that a much fuller perspective is required in order to understand both the Eucharist and the Cross. The inspiration for the approach to be presented here came from two books, by F. C. Gayford[4] and R. K. Yerkes.[5] In his book Gayford presented an interpretation of the sacrificial system of Israel and applied it to the Sacrifice of the Cross and to the Eucharist. Gayford's interpretation of Israelite sacrifice opened up the notion of sacrifice in a way that was new to the present writer, and the application to the Universal Sacrifice of Christ opened up quite startling perspectives. In the case of both Gayford and Hicks, however, the approach to the Eucharist did not fit with the Catholic understanding and so it seemed that another effort to apply these ideas was called for.

THE THREE-PART MODEL OF SACRIFICE

These writers point out that there is another model of sacrifice to be found in the Old Testament, the Temple model. In the fully developed sacrificial liturgy of Israel, described in Leviticus 1–7, there are three forms of sacrifice: the holocaust, the communion sacrifice, and the sin offering.[6] There is a wider variety of rites described in the text, there being three types of communion sacrifice and two types of sin offering, but they can be reasonably grouped under these three headings. When the structure of the Temple sacrifices is examined, one finds that there are significant differences from the simple holocaust, such as that of Noah, Abraham, or Elijah. The first point of difference is the presence of a priest who acts as the mediator between the offerer of the sacrifice and God. The other structural difference is that the Temple sacrifices end in a meal, and that means that the sacrifice takes the form of a process that unfolds in stages that can be described in summary form.[7]

The Offertory

To initiate a sacrifice, the offerer brings his offering to the priest. If it is a cereal offering, he first prepares it by pouring oil on it or adding incense, and gives it to the priest (Leviticus 2:1). If it is an animal, the offerer lays his hand on it and then kills it (1:4f.). He collects the blood and hands it to the priest (1:5). The offerer then skins the animal and cuts it up before handing it over to the priest (1:6). This ritual of offering is the same in all the sacrifices. Basically all that is happening is that the offerer prepares his gift and hands it to the priest. The word for "bringing" his gift to the priest is usually translated as "offering" it. In the LXX it is usually προσφέρειν, and the gift is often called a προσφορά.

The Priestly Mediation

The first priestly act is the ceremonial use of the blood. The blood is caught in a bowl as it leaves the victim's body and is handed at once by the offerer to the priest. The priest then performs a rite with the blood which varies according to the different kinds of sacrifice. In the holocaust and the communion sacrifices, the blood is poured against the sides of the altar (1:5; 2:2). In the sin offerings the rite is more complex. In one type, the trespass offering, the rite is the same as for the holocaust and communion sacrifice (7:2). In the sin offering for more serious offenses, some of the blood is sprinkled toward the veil of sanctuary, some is smeared on the horns of the altar, and the rest is poured at the base of the altar (4:6–7).

The Meal

The second act of the priest is to bring God's portion of the sacrifice to the altar where it is burned. For this "bringing" to the altar of God's portion by the priest, the same verb is used as for the "bringing" of his gift by the offerer to the priest, and it is also normally translated as "offering," in the LXX, again προσφέρειν. If the sacrifice is a cereal offering, the priest brings it to the altar, takes out God's portion and burns it on the altar (2:2), and the rest belongs to the priests (2:10). In an animal sacrifice, after having performed the blood rite, the priest divides up the flesh of the animal and shares it out in different ways, depending on the different sacrifices. In a holocaust the whole offering is burned on the altar (1:9). In a communion sacrifice or sin offering, the fat and certain other select portions of the carcass are burned on the altar as God's portion (3:3–5; 4:8–10). In a sin offering the priests alone may have a share (6:19), unless it is the priest himself who is making the offering, when even he cannot participate and all the remains of the carcass are burned outside the camp (4:11f.). In a communion sacrifice, though this is not mentioned anywhere in the ritual, the offerer and his guests also participate.

What has been described is the basic ritual for a sacrifice of an individual. A sacrifice could also be offered by a group. The Passover is offered by the whole people on one day, family by family, and the sin offering on the Day of Atonement was offered by the high priest in the name of the whole people. However, whether offered by an individual, by a group, or by the nation as a whole, the basic structure remains the same. The offerer of the sacrifice brings his gift of food, animal or vegetable, and offers it to God by handing it to the priest. The priest then performs his duty of priestly mediation, and distributes the food to those entitled to participate in the meal. So there is the simple three-part structure: the offertory, the priestly mediation, and the meal.

We have here, then, two models of sacrifice, each quite different from the other. The major distinguishing mark of the first, traditional, model is its unitary quality. There is no distinction between the offerer and the priest, and the priest offers the sacrifice in a single act of offering. I propose to refer to it as the "one-act" model of sacrifice. By contrast, the second model has two actors involved, the offerer and the priest, and it unfolds in the three stages, the offertory, the priestly mediation, and the meal. I propose to refer to it as the "three-part" model of sacrifice. The effort to apply the one-act model to the Eucharist has been ongoing for a thousand years, with the degree of success with which we are familiar. It is proposed now to see if the three-part model can be applied more successfully.

Even before attempting to make the application, it should be mentioned that there is a significant linguistic reason which lends support to the identification in advance. The word in Greek corresponding to the English "sacrifice" is *thusia*. The meaning, however, is not exactly the same; at least, it was not to begin with. *Thusia* did come to mean the general word "sacrifice," but originally it referred to one particular type of sacrifice. "The commonest rite in Greek religions was the *thusia*, which culminated in a common meal after a portion of the flesh had been solemnly and ceremonially burnt on an altar."[8] Like the Greeks, the Hebrews had no single word corresponding to the general use of "sacrifice" in English, and each different sacrificial rite had its own special name. Now, in the Septuagint translation of the Hebrew Bible, the word *thusia* is used to translate two of the Hebrew sacrifices, and them alone. These are the *minhah* and the *zevach*, which are the cereal and animal communion sacrifices, which share with the Greek *thusia* the common characteristic of having a common meal at the end in which all take part. It can reasonably be concluded from this that the communion sacrifice of Israel was understood to have the same structure as the Greek *thusia*. In the early Christian centuries the Eucharist was called a *thusia*, and everyone knew what a *thusia* was. "In the Greek-speaking gentile world sacrifices were still familiar. The Hellenistic world was dotted with altars and temples where *thusias* expressed the only form of worship. Every Greek in Egypt, in Asia Minor and in Greece itself, was familiar with the worship of the gods by burning steaks on an altar and participating in the feast which marked the climax of the rite."[9]

A further connection can be seen in the technical term, "sacrifice of praise." The thanksgiving communion sacrifice, whose ritual is laid down in Leviticus 7:12–15, is called by the LXX a θυσία αἰνεσέως, or sacrifice of praise, and this is the term for the Eucharist used in the Roman Canon, a *sacrificium laudis*. And even the word *eucharistia* had a background outside the Christian community. Among the Jews the communion sacrifice could be offered for three motives: the votive offering, the free will offering, and the thanksgiving sacrifice. This third, the thanksgiving sacrifice, was sometimes referred to by Philo of Alexandria as a *eucharistia*. The Greeks also offered sacrifice with different motives, one of which was thanksgiving for favors received from the gods. The technical name for such a thanksgiving sacrifice was a *eucharistia*.[10] The pattern is clear. The Greek word *thusia*, which for us is quite general, originally referred specifically to the communion sacrifice, and the Greek word *eucharistia* was in use to refer to a thanksgiving communion sacrifice well before New Testament times. These are the two words taken up by Christian tradition. Since the New Testament and Christian tradition systematically used the word *thusia* to refer to its experience of sacrifice, and the word *eucharistia* became the technical term for the Christian sacrifice before the end of the second century, it is safe to conclude that in examining the Eucharist we should be looking for the structure of a communion sacrifice.

The Three-Part Structure of the Mass

Having outlined the shape of the Old Testament sacrifice, we turn
now to applying it to the Eucharist to see if the liturgy of the Eucharist
can be recognized as a communion sacrifice. In the Eucharist there
is the sacred space defined by the altar; there is a priest who mediates
between God and the people who offer the sacrifice; there is a gift
of food, the bread and wine; and the three-part structure is there in the
Offertory, the Eucharistic Prayer, and Communion. As regards the
structure of the rite, there is not unanimity among the scholars, but
the three-part structure is proposed by Gregory Dix in his classic work
on the liturgy of the Eucharist.[11] Dix tells us that

> before the fourth century . . . [t]he outline—the Shape—of the Liturgy
> is . . . everywhere the same in all our sources, right back into the earliest
> period of which we can as yet speak with certainty, the earlier half of
> the second century.[12] . . . With absolute unanimity the liturgical tradition
> reproduces these seven actions [of our Lord at the Last Supper] as four:
> (1) The Offertory; bread and wine are "taken" and placed on the table
> together. (2) The prayer; the president gives thanks to God over the bread
> and wine together. (3) The fraction; the bread is broken. (4) The commu-
> nion; the bread and wine are distributed together. In that form and in that
> order these four actions constituted the absolutely invariable nucleus of
> every Eucharistic rite known to us throughout antiquity from the Euphrates
> to Gaul.[13]

Dix separates the Fraction and Communion as two separate parts, but
on the model we are using these would more appropriately be taken
together as the sacrificial meal. Beyond this simple summary of the
structure of the Eucharist, Dix also gives us a more elaborate description
of the details of the early Eucharist.

> All present have brought with them, each for himself or herself, a little loaf
> of bread and probably a little wine in a flask. . . . These oblations of the
> people, and any other offerings in kind which might be made, the deacons
> now bring up to the front of the altar, and arrange upon it from the
> people's side of it. The bishop rises and moves forward a few paces from the
> throne to stand behind the altar, where he faces the people with a deacon
> on either hand and his presbyters grouped around and behind him. He
> adds his own oblation of bread and wine to those of the people before him
> on the altar, and so (presumably) do the presbyters. . . . The bishop and

presbyters then laid their hands in silence upon the oblations. There followed the brief dialogue of invitation, followed by the bishop's Eucharistic prayer, which always ended with a solemn doxology, to which the people answered "Amen." . . . The bishop then broke some of the Bread and made his own communion, while the deacons broke the remainder of the Bread upon the table, and the "concelebrant" presbyters around him broke the Bread which had been held before them on little glass dishes or linen cloths by deacons during the recitation of the prayer by the bishop. . . . There followed the communion, first of the clergy, seemingly behind the altar, and then of all the people before it. . . . Such was the pre-Nicene rite.[14]

This rite can easily be interpreted to be a communion sacrifice of bread and wine. All the people bring their offerings of bread and wine, and other offerings for the support of the Church and the help of the poor. The offerings are handed to the priest, the bishop, who performs an act of priestly mediation and then the bread and wine are shared in a meal. The three-part structure is here in evidence: the offertory, the priestly mediation, and the meal. There are the two actors: the people as offerer and the priest. There are the two acts of offering: the people first offer their gifts to God into the hands of the priest, who in turn offers them to God. The Eucharistic Prayer is the act of priestly mediation, and the breaking of the bread and Communion are the priestly service of the meal.

Now, if this interpretation of the structure of the Eucharist were generally accepted, our search for the sacrificial structure of the Eucharist would be over as soon as it has begun. The similarity in structure between the communion sacrifice and the Eucharist, as here presented, is too striking to be missed. However, although Dix's book is widely recognized as a classic of liturgical studies, his structure of the Eucharist is just as widely rejected. The problem is the Offertory. The fact that the Offertory is considered to be an essential part of the Eucharist at all poses a problem for most liturgical scholars, and, in particular, the essential role of the laity in the offering of the sacrifice does not fit easily with current Eucharistic theology. It is necessary therefore to examine in detail the discussion of the Offertory and to make the case that the Offertory is indeed an essential part of the Eucharistic sacrifice.

The Argument against the Offertory[15]

The classical structure of the Eucharist, as Dix discerned it, was maintained and developed in the centuries that followed Nicaea. We will have occasion to follow that development in more detail in due course, but for the moment we need to examine briefly the background to the turn against the Offertory in Western liturgical practice and theology. Having reached a high point in the West in the ninth century, the Offertory went into decline in the tenth. And it was in the sixteenth century that the disavowal of the rite became explicit. The rejection of the Offertory among the theologians of the Reformation is well known. What is less well known, on the other hand, is that the Offertory was also rejected by Catholic theologians very soon after the Reformation. The Catholic theologians did not reject the Offertory completely, as Luther had done, but they did reject its essential role in the Eucharistic liturgy. One of the most highly influential post-Tridentine Catholic theologians was Francisco Suarez. In his study of the sacrifice of the Mass, he followed the method which had already become classic. He first of all works out his definition of a sacrifice, and then proceeds to consider the different actions of the Eucharist in turn. He observes that some theologians of the time were affirming that the Offertory formed an integral part of the Eucharist, but that none of them dared to claim it as an essential part. He then went on to give the judgment that was to become classic in Catholic theology and then, much later, in Catholic liturgical studies.

> I say, however, that this oblation pertains in no way to the substance of this sacrifice, neither as an essential part, nor as an integral part; but only as a kind of ceremonial preparation, instituted by the Church to foster devotion and reverence, inspiring the souls of the faithful in view of the mystery itself to be enacted.[16]

For this definitive judgment, he gives three reasons. His first reason is based on an interpretation of the Gospel accounts of the Last Supper which will have to be considered in due course, but of interest to us immediately is his argument based on the liturgical evidence. This second reason is that "this ceremony was not always observed by the Church, and of those things which belong to the substance or integrity of the sacrifice nothing can ever be left out."[17] His third reason is a selection of phrases and actions from the Roman Mass proving that the Offertory is preparatory and not essential. The second reason is the one we are focusing on, for it is the reason that is still dominant among liturgical scholars today.

The theologians rejected the essential role of the Offertory in the sixteenth century, but it was not until much later that the point was accepted among the liturgists. In his review of the history of the interpretation of the Eucharist among liturgists, Alan Clark tells us that up until the beginning of the twentieth century "the antiquity of the faithful's oblation was an unquestioned historical 'fact' about which no doubts had been raised by the classical school of Catholic liturgists of the seventeenth and eighteenth centuries," and that "[t]his was an inheritance from the great medieval Latin liturgists and accepted with little criticism."[18] From this we can see that though in practice the Offertory fell into abeyance in the Western Church, the basic sacrificial understanding remained in place among the liturgical scholars right into the twentieth century. Now, Clark implicitly suggests that the change to the rejection of the Offertory came as a result of "criticism," but the fact that the rejection of the Offertory had taken place in theology long before leads us to suggest an alternative interpretation of what happened.

The fact of the matter is that the first results of the historical-critical study of the early liturgy was precisely the discovery of the Offertory. This prominence of the Offertory in the early liturgy and the profoundly sacrificial character of the whole rite came as a shock and a surprise to the Protestant scholars who were first in the field, and they offered highly tendentious interpretations of what they found.[19] One of these scholars, Wetter, suggested that the prominence of the Offertory was a sure sign of the distortion by the Catholic Church of the original Christian Eucharist with sacrificial ideas drawn from the surrounding traditional religions. Surely it is not tendentious to suggest that this interpretation does not spring from a purely scholarly sifting of the evidence, but is highly influenced by the anti-sacrificial presuppositions of Protestant Eucharistic theology. On the Catholic side the determinative presuppositions were different, and Alan Clark makes no secret of his. Of Dix's interpretation of the early Eucharist as an organic action of the whole assembly, he tells us that "[t]hese views present . . . a dogmatic problem."[20] Later in the article he makes clear his view that "[t]heologically the Mass proper is circumscribed within the narrow limits of the words of Consecration spoken over the elements,"[21] and that, for him, theological considerations come first. "The theological mind tends to set it [the Offertory] aside as mere ceremonial, the popular liturgist to exaggerate its importance."[22] The "theological mind" of which Clark speaks is clearly one that is formed on the basis of the one-act model of sacrifice which centers the Eucharist completely on the priest, and on this presupposition there is obviously no place for an essential role to be granted to the Offertory. The theological problems involved here, which are very real and shared at the highest level of Catholic theology in the teaching of Pope Pius XII, will have to be dealt with in due course. However, our immediate interest is the question of the interpretation of the liturgical evidence.

It is not surprising, given the theological presuppositions, that the current argument against the Offertory is basically that outlined earlier by Suarez. Clark lays down the principle that "the function of the Offertory can be ascertained only by a comparative study of the main liturgies," and that "the nature of the Offertory Act . . . will be decided by the answer to the question, what is *done* at the Offertory at all times and in all places,"[23] and that principle cannot be faulted. Having reviewed the evidence, he states his conclusion against Dix and all who think along the same lines as follows.

Those writers who attach an overwhelming importance to the ritual oblation of the elements by the faithful and see in it the core of the "ideal" Offertory rite, are really adequately answered by the fact that such an oblation does not exist nowadays (except in one or two isolated instances) and that *as ritual* it did not exist for at least the first century of the Church's existence. In accordance with Catholic principles one would judge this particular ceremony to be subsidiary and not central.[24]

This is basically the same line of argument as put forward by Suarez three centuries earlier, though there is a significant difference. The research into the early liturgy had brought to light the role of the people in the Offertory, and so, for Clark, this role is central to the meaning of the Offertory. Clark's argument is against the "ritual oblation of the elements by the faithful," and it is based on the same two foundations as Suarez had used; one, that there was no such "ritual oblation" by the faithful in the first century, and the other that this "ritual oblation" faded out of the Roman liturgy in the second millennium. At one level, there is no debate with Clark. What he says about the "ritual oblation by the faithful" is undoubtedly true, if one takes such "ritual oblation" to mean some visible action such as an Offertory Procession, for there can be no doubt that the Offertory Procession came and went in the Roman liturgy. However, the question has to be asked whether the absence of such a "ritual oblation" implies the absence of the people's participation in the Offertory, and, following on that, the basic question remains as to whether the Offertory is an essential part of the Eucharist or not, for Clark takes his argument against the "ritual oblation by the faithful" as grounding the wider conclusion that the Offertory, and the people's participation in it, whether ritually expressed or not, cannot form an essential part of the Eucharist.

These strong denials of the people's part in the early Eucharist are not backed up by any serious analysis of the evidence available, and this fits with our suggestion that the interpretation does not spring from the evidence so much as from the theological presuppositions. Our task will be to review the evidence in some more detail than Clark has done and see if different presuppositions can provide a more plausible view of the matter. A presupposition-less interpretation of anything is impossible. The only question is as to which set of presuppositions is correct. We hope to establish that the one-act model of sacrifice is inadequate and needs to be replaced by the three-part model. We will therefore be examining the evidence with the three-part model in mind to see if it fits the evidence better, and we hope to establish that recognising the essential place of the Offertory in the Eucharist and the essential role of the people in the Offertory provides the more plausible interpretation. We will deal first with the early Eucharist and then proceed to cover the liturgical tradition until the present day.

---

1. F.C.N. Hicks, *The Fullness of Sacrifice* (London: SPCK, 1953), 327.

2. Lepin, *L'Idée du sacrifice de la Messe d'après les théologiens*, 118–121.

3. *Mediator Dei*, AAS 39 (1947), 555; § 92, *The Papal Encyclicals 1939–1958*, Claudia Carlen, IHM (Wilmington: McGrath, 1981), 134.

4. F. C. Gayford, *Sacrifice and Priesthood (Jewish and Christian)*, 2nd ed. (London: Methuen, 1953) (first ed., 1924). The original work of Gayford is summarized and developed in Hicks, *The Fullness of Sacrifice.*

5. R. K. Yerkes, *Sacrifice in Greek and Roman Religions and Early Judaism* (New York: Scribner, 1952).

6. Also helpful here was Alfred Marx, *Les offrandes végétales dans l'Ancien Testament* (Leiden/New York/Köln: E. J. Brill, 1994).

7. The short summary of the structure can be found in Gayford, *Sacrifice and the Priesthood*, 60ff., and Hicks, *The Fullness of Sacrifice*, 11ff.

8. Yerkes, *Sacrifice in Greek and Roman Religions and Early Judaism*, 92.

9. Ibid., 198–199.

10. Ibid., 102.

11. Gregory Dix, *The Shape of the Liturgy* (London: Adam and Charles Black, 1945).

12. Ibid., 5.

13. Ibid., 48.

14. Ibid., 104–5.

15. The most comprehensive version of the argument against the Offertory is to be found in Alan Clark, "The Function of the Offertory Rite in the Mass," *Ephemerides Liturgicae* 94 (1950), 309–344.

16. Disp. 75, section 3, § 1, *Opera omnia* (Paris, 1859), vol. 21, 656–7.

17. Ibid., 657.

18. Clark, "The Function of the Offertory Rite in the Mass," 312.

19. The two books were G. P. Wetter, *Altchristliche Liturgien II: Das Christliche Opfer* (Göttingen, 1922) and Hans Lietzmann, *Messe und Herrenmahl: Eine Studie zur Geschichte der Liturgie* (Berlin: Verlag Walter de Gruyter, 1926).

20. Ibid., 312.

21. Ibid., 338.

22. Ibid., 341–2.

23. Clark, "The Function of the Offertory Rite in the Mass," 320.

24. Ibid., 327.

Chapter 3

The Last Supper and the Early Eucharist

Our aim now is to examine the place of the Offertory in the early Eucharist. There is no description of the rite of the Eucharist during the first century of the Church's life, so ascertaining the role of the Offertory, if any, and that of the people requires careful analysis of the few pieces of evidence available. The argument against the essential role of the Offertory normally begins from the fact that the New Testament accounts of the Last Supper make no obvious mention of anything of the kind, so we will begin our investigation of the role of the Offertory in the early Eucharist there. An explicit statement of the position is given by Jungmann in his authoritative book on the Roman Mass. He begins his treatment of the Offertory of the Mass with his interpretation of the Last Supper.[1]

> The Master had inaugurated the Eucharistic mystery under the tokens of bread and wine—bread, such as was to be found on the table of the Last Supper, and the cup which stood before Him, these He took and changed into the heavenly gift. Bread and wine must therefore be ready at hand when the celebration of the Mass is to begin. This readying of the bread and wine need not, of course, be a ritual action. It might be taken care of, some way or other, by anyone before the beginning of the ceremonies. In the most ancient accounts, in fact, we find no traces of a special stressing of this preparatory activity.[2]

It is not mentioned explicitly, but in the context it is clear that "this preparatory activity" refers to the Offertory. Now, a large amount is being taken for granted here, and no arguments are given. The bread and wine just happen to be on the table, and the fact that "he took" them is not granted any significance at all. This presumed absence of an Offertory at the Last Supper in turn colors the interpretation of "the most ancient accounts," and since these accounts give us so little to go on, everything will turn on the interpretation of the Last Supper. In presenting no arguments, Jungmann is following in the footsteps of the man who appears to have set the pattern of the Catholic interpretation of the Last Supper, Suarez. He examined the accounts of the Last Supper to see what they would reveal about the Offertory, and concluded in peremptory fashion: "We read nothing about this in the Gospel . . . Hence, of this first action or offering, which precedes the consecration, it is simply to be denied, that Christ sacrificed with it."[3] In fact, the only argument I could find in this matter was in Luther. As part of his polemic against the Mass, he used the absence of an Offertory at the Last Supper as an argument. He wrote:

> In the third place, the words read thus: "He took the bread, thanked God, broke it and gave it to his disciples." It did not say: He took the bread and raised it up before God, to show that he had offered it to God and not given it to men. Here the counterfeits will hardly be so senseless and ignorant of the language as to dare to say that "giving to the disciples" is the same as "offering to God." Much less can "take" mean the same as "offer," when he says "he took"; for this indicates that he took the bread to himself in order to use it.[4]

In the absence of any alternative one has to assume that, without stating it, this is the argument being used by all these men. The argument is very simple. Because the Last Supper accounts do not say that Jesus raised the bread up before God, it therefore follows that they saw no sacrificial intention in the action. The comparison is with the medieval Eucharist, where the priest raised the bread up before God as a sign of offering, and its absence in the Last Supper accounts proves that no such intention was to be found there. Now, we know, as Luther did not, that the ritual action of raising the bread and wine is a late development in the Eucharistic liturgy, and to use it in an interpretation of the Last Supper accounts has to be judged anachronistic. In fact, the proper point of comparison in this context is not the medieval Mass but the form of sacrifice with which the Gospel writers and Saint Paul were familiar, that of the sacrifices of Israel. We have already presented an account of the form of Israelite sacrifice, and there is one point that is noteworthy in the present context, which is that there is no such thing there as a ritual gesture of offering. There is no raising up of the gift before God prescribed either for the offerer or the priest. The actions prescribed for each actor in the sacrifice are purely functional.

The offertory is a very simple thing. The rubrics simply say that the offerer is to bring his offering to the priest. If the offering is an animal, it must then be prepared for cooking, but if it is a cereal offering, nothing further is required at all. The "bringing to" the priest is translated into Greek as προσφέρειν, which becomes the technical word for "offering" a sacrifice in both Testaments and in Christian tradition. What constitutes the "bringing to" as "offering" is simply the context of sacrifice. It is not that there is any special "ritual action" to be performed; it is simply that food is given to God in sacrifice. We have no way of knowing what ritual may have accompanied this act, what prayers were said, what psalms were sung. On a busy day in the Temple a procession would have formed in the way that a queue will form when any group of people have to perform an action in turn. However, none of this is essential. All that is required is that the occasion be a sacrifice, and that food is being offered to God for this purpose. The same simplicity of offering applies to the actions of the priest. He has to deal with the flesh and blood of the animal or with the bread and wine of a cereal offering, but what constitutes this work as "offering" is simply the "bringing to" the altar that it requires. No ritual actions are prescribed to express the fact that the action is an "offering" or a "giving" of the gift to God. This is obvious from the context of sacrifice. Again, we have no way of knowing what ritual actions may or may not have accompanied the actions to be performed, but what is important is that they are not necessary to indicate the significance of what was happening. The significance comes from the context, the context of sacrifice.

The interpretation of the Last Supper accounts depends, therefore, on the context in which they are read. Was the Last Supper a sacrifice? If so, what kind of a sacrifice was it? It is only when we have answers to those prior questions that we can have any real hope of knowing what is meant. The accounts are so bare that it is simply impossible to interpret them without an overall context. And how is that context to be established? Everything is going to depend on the presuppositions with which one approaches the text. "What characterises Catholic exegesis is that it deliberately places itself within the living tradition of the Church, whose first concern is fidelity to the revelation attested by the Bible."[5] Now, the central core of the living tradition of the Church is precisely the Eucharist, and it must, therefore, be recognized as the most authoritative commentary on the scriptural accounts of the Last Supper. Luther used the details of the medieval Mass to interpret the details of the Last Supper, and that was anachronistic and wrong. But it is quite a different matter to use the meaning of the Eucharist throughout the centuries to interpret the meaning of the Last Supper. In this connection, Dom Gregory Dix has important points to make. He writes:

> [I]t is important for the understanding of the whole future history of the liturgy to grasp the fact that Eucharistic worship from the outset was not based on Scripture at all, whether of the Old or New Testament, but solely on *tradition*. The authority for its celebration was the historical tradition that it had been instituted by Jesus, cited incidentally by St Paul in 1 Cor 11 and attested in the second Christian generation by the written Gospels. The method of celebrating it, the primitive outline of the liturgy, was from the first prescribed, not by an authoritative code, but by the tradition of custom alone.[6]

Later, after having described how the seven-action scheme of the Last Supper became the four-action scheme of the Eucharist, he goes on:

> This unanimity with which the early liturgical tradition runs *counter* to the statements of the New Testament documents that our Lord took, blessed and distributed the bread separately from the cup, and broke the bread before He blessed the cup, is curious. . . . Evidently, liturgical practice was not understood by the primitive Church to be in any way subject to the control of the NT documents, even when these had begun to be regarded as inspired Scripture. This liturgical tradition must have originated in independence of the literary tradition in all its forms, Pauline or Synoptic. And it must have been very solidly established everywhere as the invariable practice before the first three Gospels began to circulate with authority. . . .[7]

The significance of this is that it is the Eucharist that gives us the meaning of what our Lord did at the Last Supper. It follows that it does not make sense for us to ignore the Eucharist and go back to the bare texts in search of any possible alternative interpretation.[8] As Saint Cyprian argued, what our Lord did at the Last Supper, he

commanded the apostles to "do this" in his memory. The practice of
the Eucharist down the centuries is the infallibly guaranteed fulfilment
of that command. The basic argument in favor of interpreting our
Lord's "taking" of the bread and wine as being the offertory of the
Last Supper sacrifice is simply this correspondence with the Eucharist.
If the Eucharist is the fulfilment of the command to "do this," then
the "taking" must correspond to the Offertory. It would be better,
all the same, if this interpretation could be grounded in the context of
the Last Supper itself, and, in fact, there are considerations which can
be brought forward in favor of it.

The Last Supper as a Communion Sacrifice of Bread and Wine

In the first place, we know, from the teaching of Tradition, authorita-
tively confirmed at the Council of Trent, that Christ offered a sacrifice
at the Last Supper, and the sacrifice was a sacrifice of bread and
wine, according to the order of Melchizedech. Once that point is taken
as given, the interpretation of Old Testament sacrifice we are using
here allows certain conclusions to be drawn. Taking it, then, that the
Last Supper sacrifice was a sacrifice in the Old Testament tradition,
we can conclude that it must have been a communion sacrifice, for that
is the only one in the Israelite system where all the participants join in
the meal, which all did at the Last Supper. An interesting text in
corroboration of this is Psalm 116:17, one of the Hallel psalms sung at
Passover, where it says, "I will offer you a thanksgiving sacrifice." The
thanksgiving sacrifice is precisely the name given to the communion
sacrifice offered in thanks to God which is described in Leviticus 7:12ff.
We are entitled to expect, therefore, that the structure of the communion sacrifice would be verified in the sacrifice offered at the Last
Supper, and we should expect to find an offertory, which is the first
stage of every sacrifice.

The Last Supper as a Passover Sacrifice

Another essential point to be established is whether or not the Last
Supper sacrifice was a Passover. In modern scholarship there is doubt
about this, despite the clear statement of intent by our Lord himself,

that "I have eagerly longed to eat this Passover with you before
I suffer" (Luke 22:15). And it is not only this single verse that indicates
that the Last Supper sacrifice was a Passover. In the context of the
overall theology of Christ's saving work it must have been. Nothing
else makes sense. Time and time again in his preaching and his
miracles our Lord made clear that he was fulfilling the prophecy of the
Exodus. He was the New Moses and the New Jesus (Joshua) leading
the people into the Promised Land. To make sense of that, he had
to celebrate the Passover. He was fulfilling all the sacrifices of Israel, and
this is the most important of all. It is simply theologically unthinkable
that the Last Supper was not a Passover. This faith conviction has to
face two problems arising from the chronology of the first Holy Week
that must be addressed, for, without a solid conviction that the Last
Supper was a Passover, our interpretation of the rite cannot get off the
ground, since the interpretation of the text demands a solidly established
context. It is necessary, therefore, to undertake a rather lengthy
digression to clarify this matter once and for all.

The Chronology of the Last Supper

The Johannine view of the matter is clear: Our Lord was crucified on
14 Nisan, the day before the Passover. The Passover supper of the Jews
is celebrated on the eve of 15 Nisan and the lambs for the supper
are killed on the afternoon before, on 14 Nisan. Saint John specifies
the day of the Crucifixion in various places. He says of the Jewish
leaders that "they themselves did not enter the praetorium, so as to
avoid ritual defilement and to be able to eat the Passover" (John 18:28).
Of that day he says, "Now it was the day of Preparation for the
Passover" (19:14) and "since it was the day of Preparation" (19:31).
His account makes clear that our Lord was being crucified at precisely
the same time that the lambs were being slaughtered in the Temple.
This chronology is corroborated by the early tradition of the
Quartodecimans. These were the early Jewish Christians whose folk
memory of the events cannot be seriously questioned. From the
earliest days Jewish Christians in Jerusalem normally joined with their
countrymen in observing 14 Nisan as the day our Lord died.[9] Irenaeus
says, "Anicetus could not persuade Polycarp not to observe, seeing
that he had always observed with John the disciple of our Lord and

the rest of the apostles with whom he had associated."[10] However, this apparently impregnable tradition was questioned in the second century, and the resulting controversy has not yet been resolved.

Great dispute broke out in Laodicea in the decade 160–170, where some people began using the Synoptic chronology to oppose the usage hitherto accepted. Apollinaris of Hierapolis reports: "And they say that on the 14th the Lord ate the sheep with the disciples and Himself suffered on the Great Day of Unleavened Bread; and they argue that Matthew speaks as they have supposed; hence their opinion is inconsistent with the Law, and the Gospels seem, according to them, to be at variance."[11] The idea is that since the Synoptics affirm clearly that the meal was a Passover, it cannot have taken place on the previous day, before the lambs had been killed. Indeed, it has to be conceded that if our Lord "ate the sheep," his death cannot have been synchronized with the slaughter of the lambs in the Temple, as Saint John reports. Not many of the documents from the controversy have survived, but one very important witness has come down to us.

> Clement of Alexandria . . . resting his case on the Fourth Gospel and explaining that the Synoptics speak with the same voice, argued that Christ did not eat the legal Passover meal, but died on the 14th day, being himself the true Paschal Victim.[12]

Clement of Alexandria makes two very important affirmations here. He claims "that the Synoptics speak with the same voice" as Saint John and "that Christ did not eat the legal Passover meal," and both need to be examined with care. Can his first contention be sustained, "that the Synoptics speak with the same voice"? In fact, on the issue of pure chronology, the Synoptics can be interpreted as agreeing with Saint John. Saint Mark opens his account of the Last Supper: "On the first day of Unleavened Bread, when the Passover lamb is sacrificed" (Mark 14:12). Specifying that it was the day the lambs were killed makes clear that Saint Mark had 14 Nisan in mind. And it can be taken that the meal was eaten on that day, therefore on the evening before, if Mark's account is interpreted as follows: In the Jewish calendar the day begins at sunset the previous evening. The disciples were sent to prepare the Upper Room, but our Lord told them: "He will show you a large room upstairs, furnished and ready. Make preparations for us there" (Mark 14:15). So, the preparations would not have been elaborate and could easily fit into the period of daylight between sunset and darkness, "between the two evenings" of 14 Nisan, as Saint John states clearly. If the preparations had taken place during the *day* of 14 Nisan and the meal in the evening, then the meal would have taken place on 15 Nisan and Saint Mark's heading would be inaccurate. So, a reasonable interpretation of the Synoptic chronology allows for unanimity with Saint John on that score, and an interpretation that avoids contradiction between the Gospels should be accepted, and Clement of Alexandria judged to be correct.

However, the more important difficulty remains. This is the problem created by the fact that the Synoptics are clear that the Last Supper was a Passover meal, and a Passover on the eve of 14 Nisan is, apparently at least, impossible. How could a Passover be celebrated on the evening *before* the lambs were killed in the Temple, since a properly killed lamb from the Temple was essential to the rite? So is Clement of Alexandria correct in his other contention, that "Christ did not eat the legal Passover meal"? Joachim Jeremias, in his thorough analysis of this whole question, treats the possibility of an anticipated Passover with peremptory disdain. He notes that it corresponds to the tradition of the Eastern Church and is espoused by a few named exegetes and then simply asserts that it is impossible.[13] In a footnote he carries the discussion slightly further and rejects it again on the ground that it is against the Law of Moses. Now, both of these objections are true up to a point, but they can both be turned around in ways that Jeremias does not consider.

The breach of the Mosaic Law is, indeed, a serious matter, but it does not of itself render the anticipated Passover out of the question. In fact, it fits a pattern of behavior which our Lord chose deliberately in other areas. He showed his Messianic superiority over the *Torah* by his breach of the Sabbath, and the possibility cannot be overlooked that the same attitude is being evidenced in this case also. One of the exegetes Joachim Jeremias refers to makes this point precisely.

> But the Passover was deliberately changed. As the Lord's Supper is a completely new Supper, so he chose a new time to celebrate the Passover. . . . for he is the Messiah who brings the new order founded by God. . . .
> In Mark the prediction and its fulfilment is certainly presented as a miracle, just as at the Entry into Jerusalem (11:3). . . . The Lord's special knowledge

and preparations fit the special character of this Last Supper, and the process of the miracle highlights the fact that God Himself is at work here.[14]

If the breach of the Mosaic Law does not present an insurmountable difficulty, what form could such an anticipated Passover take? What is clearly impossible is the celebration of the traditional Passover with a lamb from the Temple on 14 Nisan since the lambs were all killed during the (Roman) day following, and this is presumably the impossibility Jeremias has in mind. But what about the possibility of celebrating the Passover *without a lamb from the Temple*? Such a celebration would have been unprecedented, but would it have been impossible? That the celebration was of this kind is the considered opinion of another serious student of the question.

Given the absence of any reference to the lamb in the Synoptic accounts, either in the preparation or in the supper itself, it is perhaps prudent to stay with the hypothesis that the Last Supper of Jesus was a supper without the paschal lamb, and still a "paschal" supper, not so much in that it was according to the ancient rite, but rather that it was the new Passover and the Synoptics wished to emphasize this fact.[15]

These two suggestions taken together lead to the interpretation being proposed here, that our Lord, with full consciousness of the implications involved, deliberately chose to celebrate the Passover without a lamb from the Temple.

To see how this suggestion fits with the overall Synoptic presentation of the events of Holy Week a number of points need to be made. In the first place, as Schniewind points out, it is clearly brought out that the events of the Week have been carefully prepared. When the two disciples are sent ahead to find the animal on which our Lord will ride into Jerusalem, his predictions as to how it will work out need not be seen as a form of mini-prophecy, but rather an indication that our Lord has made his preparations well in advance and that he has come to Jerusalem for this final Passover with a definite goal in mind. It is, further, very relevant that the triumphal entry into Jerusalem leads directly to the purging of the Temple. It is more often than not presumed that the driving of the buyers and sellers out of the Temple is simply a prophetic gesture of criticism of the Temple worship. However, a deeper significance would seem to fit better with the solemnity of the occasion of the triumphal entry of the Messiah into Jerusalem. It would seem to be more likely that our Lord, rather than offering a prophetic critique of the Temple worship, is giving symbolic expression to his Messianic decree of its abolition and replacement by his own new sacrificial system. A short perusal of Synoptic commentaries has found no corroboration of such a suggestion, but it is to be found among the Johannine scholars.

> The purging of the temple—that is, the expulsion of the sacrificial animals from its courts—signifies the destruction and replacement of the system of religious observance of which the temple was the centre: a new "temple" for an old one.[16]

The close association in John of the purging of the Temple with the marriage feast of Cana, which so clearly predicts the complete renewal of the Jewish religion, makes the deeper significance more apparent.

> In each case he makes the same point—the old Jewish order is to be replaced by what is quite new in himself. The water of Jewish purification . . . is to be replaced by the new wine of the Gospel, i.e., by the self-sacrifice of the Lamb of God. The sacrificial worship of the temple, particularly the great festival of Passover, is to be replaced by a new spiritual worship offered first by and then through him who will suffer the destruction of the temple of his body only to erect it anew in his resurrection.[17]

This radical interpretation of the cleansing of the Temple is supported by the texts surrounding it in the Synoptic gospels. Mark places it between the cursing and withering of the fig tree, with its obvious reference to the replacement of the Old Israel with the New. The questioning of Jesus' authority in the cleansing of the Temple is followed by the parable of the wicked tenants with its message of the replacement of the old leaders of Israel with the new. The next chapter foretells the destruction of the Temple as part of the eschatological discourse.

This, then, is the background to the preparations for the Passover. Our Lord sends two of his disciples ahead to make preparation for the Passover. As at the entry he tells them what they will find, and in this instance Mark makes it clear that the room has already been prepared. "He will show you a large room upstairs, furnished and ready" (Mark 14:15). He has already indicated that this is taking place on the day "when the Passover lamb is killed," so that it would be quite impossible for the provision of one of the Temple lambs to have been part of their preparations. And how could it have been in any case? Our Lord had symbolically driven the buyers and sellers of the lambs out of the Temple on Palm Sunday. How then could he have sent his disciples to deal with them on Holy Thursday to acquire a lamb for the Passover, even if it were possible? No; the whole context demands that there was no lamb from the Temple at the Last Supper, and Clement of Alexandria is correct again that "Christ did not eat the legal Passover meal."

On this reading, the "impossibility" of celebrating the traditional Passover ceases to be a problem to be solved and becomes, rather, a central point of the Synoptic account. The Synoptic writers were familiar with the Jewish Passover and they knew well that a Passover celebrated in anticipation could not possibly be celebrated with a lamb from the Temple. Their insistence that it was celebrated the evening before the lambs were killed was precisely to make clear that the celebration was without such a lamb. In this way they were pointing to the fact that the only lamb at this New Passover was the New Lamb of God, Jesus himself.

The Offertory of the Last Supper

Two aspects of the Last Supper have been established. It was a communion sacrifice of bread and wine, and it was the New Passover where the New Lamb, Jesus himself, was eaten. Putting these two together, the conclusion emerges that the Last Supper sacrifice was a sacramental sacrifice, a communion sacrifice of bread and wine which was sacramentally the New Passover of the new and eternal Covenant. In this context, it comes as no surprise that there are differences in the Synoptic accounts from the normal Passover liturgy. The form of the sacrifice was not the Passover, but a communion sacrifice of thanksgiving, a *Eucharist,* so bitter herbs do not come into it any more than the legal lamb. The choice of leavened bread could have been deliberate to emphasize the point that the ceremony was not a legal Passover. But two of the differences were surely significant. The old Passover was a family celebration, and Jesus chose to celebrate it with his apostles, his new family, the Church. The whole people of Israel celebrated the Passover together, and the new people of the New Israel were now beginning the celebration of the New Passover which will last forever. And again, at the old Passover, individual cups were used, whereas at Jesus' New Passover, one chalice was shared among them all, because they were all drinking the one cup of suffering, the one that Jesus himself drank. This connection between the Last Supper and the Cross follows from the fact that the Lamb shared at the Supper was the Lamb who would be slain the following day.

All this is essential background when we come to consider the question of the offertory of the Last Supper sacrifice. In the case of the Passover, in particular, the situation is simpler yet, because the Passover was a traditional sacrifice in Israel before the Temple was built and the priest has no essential role to play in its performance, so that even the "bringing to" the priest does not form part of the ceremony. The relevant rubric for the Passover sacrifice is expressed once and once only in the Old Testament, in the book of Exodus, and the instruction could not be simpler. "They shall take each man a lamb . . . one for each family . . . then, with the whole assembly of Israel present, it shall be slaughtered during the evening twilight" (Exodus 12:3–6). Moses repeats the instruction in verse 21: "Go and take a lamb according to your families and sacrifice the Passover." Again, we have no way of knowing what "ritual actions" might have accompanied the "taking" of the Passover lamb, but none of it is essential to the reality that a lamb is here being "offered" to God in sacrifice and that it is being offered by the whole of Israel, family by family. Exactly the same is to be said of our Lord's action at the Last Supper. He "took" the bread and wine and offered them to God in sacrifice, and he was "taking" and offering them on behalf of the whole group of himself and his apostles as representatives of the whole New People of God. The two essential points here, from the point of view of the present discussion, are that the "taking" of the bread and wine is all that is required to constitute the offertory of the Passover sacrifice, and that the offering is made on behalf of the group, as is in the nature of the Passover. This communal nature of the offering is also made clear by the manner in which the Last Supper was prepared. Our Lord gave instructions to the apostles to prepare the Supper. The food required was, therefore, purchased from the common fund and was the property of the group, so that the offering was made by our Lord as head of the group on behalf of all, just as the head of the family offered the old Passover on behalf of his whole family.

This essential communal dimension of the offertory at the Last Supper is confirmed when we consider another aspect of the sacrifice, since we further know by faith that the Eucharist is not simply the New Passover, but a sin offering as well. Our Lord said as much in his words of blessing over the chalice, that his blood was being shed "for the forgiveness of sins" (Matthew 26:28). And the Council of Trent teaches that "If anyone says that the sacrifice of the Mass is . . . not a propitiatory sacrifice . . . *anathema sit*" (DS 1753/ND 1557). This must be taken to mean that, in his Last Supper sacrifice, he was fulfilling the national sin offering made annually by the whole people on the Day of Atonement. The fulfilment of this sacrifice on the Cross is made clear by the teaching of the Letter to the Hebrews, but it stands to reason that our Lord had it in mind that the new sacrifice he was instituting for his Church would fulfill this sacrifice along with all the rest.

These points are all relevant when we come to consider the offertory of the Last Supper sacrifice. The Passover and the national sin offering are unique in the sacrificial system in that they are offered by the whole nation, the Passover family by family, the national sin offering by the whole people together, led by the high priest. In the national sin offering, the only one active is the high priest: He performs the offertory alone, for himself, his family, and the whole people. And yet it is clear that he is acting on behalf of everyone. "From the Israelite community he shall receive two male goats for a sin offering (Leviticus 16:5) . . . *Taking* the two male goats and setting them before the Lord at the entrance of the meeting tent (16:7) . . . The goat that is determined by lot for the Lord, Aaron shall bring in and offer up as a sin offering" (16:9). The high priest performs the actions, but the offering is that of the people. From this we can see that to offer a sacrifice it is not necessary to make any specific gesture of offering, or to be active at all in the offertory process. What matters is to whom the victim belongs, on whose behalf it is being offered. In the Last Supper accounts, it speaks of our Lord "taking the bread," and "taking the cup," just as Leviticus invariably speaks of the priest "taking" the victim to perform his priestly work. One can see, then, that just as

the high priest "took" the offering on behalf of the whole nation,
so Christ, at the Last Supper, "took" the offering on behalf of his new
People, offering sacramentally the Universal Sacrifice for the salvation
of the whole world. He "took" the bread and wine, but the offering
was that of the whole People of God. All this confirms the conclusion
that when Christ "took" the bread and wine he was performing the
Offertory of the first Eucharist. And it does more. It clarifies the role
of the people in the Offertory. Just as the Last Supper was offered
by and for the whole People, so also is the Eucharist. The priest acts in
the person of Christ in offering the sacrifice, but the offering is that of
the whole Church.

MATTHEW 5:23–24

Before leaving the New Testament it is necessary to consider a text
from Matthew's Gospel, which is very closely associated with the
Offertory in the Tradition.

> Therefore, if you are offering your gift (προσφέρῃς τὸ δῶρον σου) at
> the altar, and there remember that your brother has anything against you,
> leave your gift at the altar, go and be reconciled with your brother first,
> and then come and offer your gift. (Matthew 5:23–24)

This text forms a bridge which carries us all the way from the public
life of our Lord to the redaction of the Gospel well into the first century
and beyond, owing to its use in all the early liturgies in immediate
association with the Offertory. This text, in fact, is the origin of the
rite of the Kiss of Peace, which originally was a preparation for the
Offertory. "Justin is the first author who actually states that the kiss of
peace is the preliminary to the offertory, where we find the kiss placed
also by Hippolytus at Rome some sixty years later. It was evidently
a fixed and settled part of the liturgical tradition that it should come at
this point of the rite at Rome as elsewhere in pre-Nicene times."[18] In
the *Sitz im Leben* of the preaching of our Lord himself, the reference
must be to the Temple sacrifices in Jerusalem. His hearers were all Jews
and were regular in their sacrificial worship, and they must have
understood his teaching in that context, as referring to their offering
of their sacrifices in the Temple. Its redaction into the Sermon on
the Mount places precisely the same teaching in the context of the

apostolic preaching. And, finally, the entry of the meaning of the
text into all the early liturgies as the Kiss of Peace before the Offertory
indicates that Christians understood what they were doing in the
Eucharist in this context. Can we not reasonably conclude that the
apostles and the early Christians understood their worship as being
continuous with the Temple worship they had known, at least in
this regard? The teaching fits both contexts perfectly and there is no
sense at all of the Christian setting requiring any radically different
interpretation. We take it from this that the early Christians understood
themselves to be "offering their gift at the altar" in the Eucharist, and
that this understanding of the Offertory as being something belonging
to the people also, which was to become so obvious in the later liturgies,
is present here from the very earliest days. It is also evidence of the
understanding of Christian sacrifice as being in substantial continuity
with the sacrifices of Israel which would only be made explicit by
Saint Irenaeus two centuries later. From the point of view of the argument being developed here, it corroborates the two essential points,
that the Offertory formed an essential part of the Eucharist and that
the Offertory was performed by the people, whether or not it received
any ritual expression. On this basis we deem that the peremptory
judgment of another influential liturgical scholar stands corrected, who
wrote in the article which set the tone of interpretation in Catholic
liturgical studies since: "The New Testament does not imply in any
way the existence of a food offering, either as an independent
ceremony or as a rite preparatory to the Last Supper."[19] The Offertory
may not be "an independent ceremony" or "a rite preparatory to the
Last Supper," but the implied denial of any role cannot be allowed to
stand. We have presented strong evidence in favor of the assertion that
it forms an essential part of both the Last Supper and the early
Eucharist, as it must form an essential part of any sacrifice.

---

1. Joseph A. Jungmann, sj, *The Mass of the Roman Rite: Its Origins and Development*, vol. two (New York, 1955), 1–2.

2. Ibid., 1.

3. Disp. 75, section 2, § 2, *Opera omnia* (Paris, 1859), vol. 21, 654.

4. Martin Luther, "The Misuse of the Mass" (1522), in Abdel Ross Wentz, editor, and Helmut Lehmann, general editor, *Luther's Works* Volume 36 (Philadelphia: Fortress Press, 1959), 133–223, at 170.

5. Pontifical Biblical Commission, *The Interpretation of the Bible in the Church* (Rome: Libreria Editrice Vaticana, 1993), 85.

6. Dix, *The Shape of the Liturgy*, 3.

7. Ibid., 49.

8. The alternative approach which presumes an evolution from a primitive to a later, quite different, form is clearly dealt with in another context by David Albert Jones, OP, in "Was there a Bishop of Rome in the First Century?" *New Blackfriars*, March 1999, 128–143, and "The Bishop of Rome Revisited," *New Blackfriars*, June 1999, 309–312.

9. W. H. Cadman, "The Christian Pascha and the Day of the Crucifixion," *Studia Patristica V, Texte und Untersuchungen 80*, Berlin 1962, 8–16, at 8.

10. Eusebius *Hist. Eccl.* V 23-25, quoted in Cadman, "The Christian Pascha and the Day of the Crucifixion," 9.

11. Cadman, "The Christian Pascha and the Day of the Crucifixion," 13.

12. Quoted from fragments preserved in the *Chron. Pasch*. I, in Dindorf's edition (Bonn, 1832, 12–15), Cadman, 14.

13. Joachim Jeremias, *The Eucharistic Words of Jesus* (London: SCM, 1966), 21.

14. Julius Schniewind, *Das Evangelium nach Markus: Das Neue Testament Deutsch*, (Göttingen, 1959), 146.

15. Raniero Cantalamessa, *La Pasqua della nostra salvezza. Le tradizioni pasquali della Bibbia e della primitiva chiesa.* (Marietti: Casale Monferrato, 1971), 97.

16. C. H. Dodd, *The Interpretation of the Fourth Gospel* (Cambridge: Cambridge University Press, 1968), 301.

17. John Marsh, *Saint John* (Penguin, 1968), 164.

18. Dix, *The Shape of the Liturgy*, 108.

19. J. Coppens, "L'Offrande des fidèles dans la Liturgie eucharistique ancienne," *Cours et conférences des semaines liturgiques* (Louvain: Mont-César), t. V (1927), 99–123, at p. 107.

Chapter 4

The Offertory in Tradition

Having presented an alternative interpretation of the place of the offertory in the Last Supper sacrifice, and the role in it of the people, represented by the apostles, we need now to examine the tradition of the Eucharist to see if this interpretation is corroborated by the evidence available. The first mention of a "ritual act" of offering is found in Saint Justin in the second century, and the argument against the significance of this act is grounded in the fact that no ritual act of offering is to be found in the texts from the first century of the Church's life. Coppens reports a complete "silence among the Apostolic Fathers: never the least trace of a liturgical offering nor, *a fortiori*, of any connection between such a rite and the celebration of the Eucharist."[1] We have already made the point in discussing the Last Supper that in the tradition of Israelite sacrifice, there is no such thing as a ritual act of offering, so that its absence need not be a crucial point in the interpretation of early texts. It has to be conceded that there is no explicit mention of a liturgical rite of offering, but whether or not it is true to say that there is no trace whatever of offering in the texts is another question entirely. With the presuppositions that we have established it may be possible to find references that might otherwise pass unnoticed. So let us examine the few texts that are available and see what they reveal.

THE *DIDACHE*

The first text available is one written around the same time as Saint Matthew's Gospel (50–70 AD), the *Didache*:

> On the Lord's own day, assemble in common to break bread and offer thanks (εὐχαριστησατε) ; but first confess your sins, so that your sacrifice (ἡ θυσία ὑμῶν) may be pure. However, no one quarrelling with his

brother may join your meeting until they are reconciled; your sacrifice (θυσία) must not be defiled (cf. Matt 5:23f.). For here we have the saying of the Lord: "In every place and time offer me a pure sacrifice (θυσία); for I am a mighty king, says the Lord; and my name spreads terror among the nations" (Malachi 1:11, 14).[2]

This is the first time the Eucharist is openly called a sacrifice. As one recent commentator points out: "The concept of a sacrifice is introduced neither apologetically, as if there had been alternative opinions in the community to be corrected, nor polemically, as if one had to defend the notion of the Eucharist as sacrifice against distortion or denial. . . . And it is 'your sacrifice,' with the clear implication that it is the offering of the people that is meant."[3] A small but important point is at stake here, for there has been a shift in the understanding of the word "sacrifice" over the centuries. For us, the word refers primarily to the rite, the whole action of the sacrifice. We think first of a sacrifice as a liturgical event. Originally, however, the primary referent was not the rite but the gift: The "sacrifice" was what was offered. And so it is in this case. "*Didache* 14 understands by θυσία specifically the sacrificial gifts. . . . In Malachi 1:11 θυσία refers to the gifts . . . [and] the reference to Matthew 5:23f. makes the parallel θυσία—δῶρόν."[4] These few considerations make clear the points that are of interest for our purposes here, that the Eucharist is understood to be a sacrifice in the traditional sense, and that the people's offering is understood to be an essential part of it.

SAINT CLEMENT OF ROME

Let us move forward a few years to the end of the first century and consider a text from Pope Saint Clement of Rome's *First Letter to the Corinthians.*

> § 40. Since all these things are clear to us, and we have looked into the depths of divine knowledge, we ought in proper order to do all things which the Lord has commanded us to perform at appointed times. He has commanded the offerings (προσφορὰς) and liturgies (λειτουργίας) to be carried out, and not carelessly or disorderly, but at fixed times and seasons. He has Himself fixed according to His surpassing counsel where and by whom He desires them to be performed, in order that all things may be done in holy fashion according to His good pleasure and acceptable

to His will. Those who make their offerings (ποιοῦτες τασ προσφορὰς) at the appointed time, therefore, are acceptable and blessed, for they err not, following the ordinances of the Lord. For the High Priest has been allotted his proper ministrations, and to the priests their proper place has been assigned, and on the Levites their own duties are laid. The layman is bound by the lay ordinances.

§ 41. Let us, brothers, each in his own order, strive to please God with a good conscience and with reverence, not transgressing the fixed rule of each one's own ministry. Not in every place, brothers, are the daily sacrifices for petitions and for sins and for trespasses offered (προσφέρονται θυσίαι), but only in Jerusalem. And even there the offering is not made in any place, but only before the sanctuary near the altar, after the offering has been inspected by the High Priest and the above-mentioned ministers. Those who do anything contrary to what is due to Him will suffer the penalty of death. You see, brothers, the more knowledge we have been given, the more we are exposed to danger.[5]

This presentation of the Eucharist from the first century could hardly be more sacrificial in its tone. It uses all the language of the Old Testament sacrifices, and even speaks as if the Christian worship were taking place in the Temple in Jerusalem. There is no mention of any Offertory rite, but it speaks of the offerings which are to be made, and how each rank in the Church, bishops, priest, deacons, and laity, has its own liturgical function in the Eucharist. One commentator on Pope Saint Clement's Letter has this to say: "In the offering of the Eucharistic sacrifice, in fact, the role of the *laity* does not appear as purely passive. It is their offering (44, 4) which the High Priest and the *'hiéreis'* transfer to God in *their* place. The Eucharistic liturgy is not only the liturgy of the 'hierarchy'—rather these [the laity] have *an irreplaceable role*, without which the celebration of the liturgy is impossible—it is the liturgy of *the Church, the Priestly People, the Body of Christ 'hierarchically' constituted.* And *all* have their role, but each 'in his place' (41, 1) according to *'the rules imposed by his office,'* in an organic and *hierarchic* celebration of the liturgy."[6] Here again, there is no mention of any "ritual act" of offering, but the role of the laity in offering the sacrifice is made abundantly clear. It represents a complete corroboration of Dix's picture of the ideal Eucharist, celebrated according to a liturgy in complete continuity with the sacrificial liturgy of Israel.

SAINT JUSTIN MARTYR

And so we arrive at the texts of Saint Justin Martyr where the Offertory of the Eucharist is first mentioned explicitly. However, we now have a background established which will enable us to examine somewhat more carefully the opinions put forward in regard to these texts. Our aim has been to counter the opinion that fails to see a sacrifice in the early Eucharist and, correspondingly, sees no particular significance in Saint Justin's account of the Offertory. The main protagonist here is Jungmann.[7] In his account of the story, he puts forward the view that the early Eucharist was not a sacrifice, but rather "a prayer of thanks connected with a meal,"[8] and he attributes this understanding to Saint Justin. He argues that the earliest understanding of the Eucharist "excluded the notion that a true and genuine oblation to God could be discerned in the gifts of bread and wine which were placed on the table for the Eucharist, or in those things presented by the faithful for the agape or for alms. This view Justin holds quite firmly."[9] According to Jungmann, Saint Justin "holds quite firmly" that the Eucharist is not a sacrifice, and that affirmation needs to be examined. Let us first of all quote at somewhat greater length the text of the *First Apology* in question.

> Having ended the prayers, we salute one another with a kiss. There is then brought to (προσφέρεται) to the president of the brethren bread and a cup of wine mixed with water; and he taking (λαβὼν) them, gives praise and glory to the Father . . . and offers thanks (εὐχαριστίαν) . . . And when the president has given thanks . . . those who are called by us deacons give to each of those present to partake of the bread and wine mixed with water over which the thanksgiving was pronounced (εὐχαριστηθέντος).[10]

Let us now consider how Dix presents the same text.

> Justin says, "When we have ended (the intercessions) we salute one another with a kiss. Then bread is 'offered' (*prospheretai*) to the president and a cup of water mingled with wine." (*Apology 1*, 65) . . . he knows the technical meaning of *prospheretai* interpreting Mal 1:11; "In every place incense shall be offered unto My name and a pure *offering*" as referring to the Eucharist. He explains the last words as "The sacrifices which are offered (*prospheromenon*) to God by us gentiles, that is the bread of the Eucharist and cup likewise of the Eucharist." (*Dialogue*, 41) . . . he is quite clear

that there is a real "offering" in the rite, specifically of the bread and wine; and he uses this technical word for the liturgical offering.[11]

The crucial point here is the interpretation of *prospheretai*. Is the word being used in its straightforward sense of "brought to," as Jungmann understands it, or in its technical sacrificial sense of "offered," as does Dix? In favor of the technical sense, Dix brings forward evidence from other parts of Saint Justin's writings. And Dix is not alone in this interpretation. For instance, another commentator on these patristic texts who has no particular sympathy for the sacrificial interpretation of the Eucharist, summarizes the matter as follows.

> When speaking of pagan, Jewish and Christian sacrifice, Justin used indiscriminately the same sacrificial terms such as θυσία, σπονδή, προσφορά, προσφέρειν, etc. O. Casel is quite right in pointing out that this usage indicates that Justin considered Christian sacrifice as belonging to the same genus as pagan sacrifice and Jewish sacrifice. Although he was continually insisting on the essential difference between them, Justin clearly thought that what Christians offered was real sacrifice.[12]

It appears that the exegetes are evenly divided on this,[13] so it hardly seems useful for the effort to settle the exegetical question to be undertaken here. Our presentation of the sacrificial tradition of Israel and the meaning of all these words in Christian Tradition leaves us in no doubt as to which side of the argument is to be chosen. However, a further argument can be brought forward on the broader level of the coherence of the Christian Tradition. Immediately after his affirmation about Saint Justin's understanding of the Eucharist, Jungmann continues: "Tertullian has watered it down. But Irenaeus plainly takes a new stand. In explaining the Eucharist, he emphasised the fact that we offer the firstlings of creation."[14] According to Jungmann, therefore, a radical change in the understanding of the Eucharist took place between Saint Justin and Saint Irenaeus. We suggest that such a hypothesis is unacceptable, given the infallibility of the Church. An interpretation of Saint Justin that implies a radical break with subsequent Tradition can only be seriously entertained if the evidence for it is clear and incontrovertible. We have enough evidence at hand already to be quite certain that such is not the case. There is a plain, straightforward interpretation of Saint Justin that makes his position completely compatible with Irenaeus and the whole of the subsequent Catholic

Tradition, and we suggest that this is the interpretation that must
be chosen.

Taking it, then, that the sacrificial interpretation of Saint
Justin is a reasonable option, let us consider what he says about the
Offertory. Jungmann has an opinion about this as well. Speaking
of the role of the Offertory in the early Eucharist, he says: "In the most
ancient accounts, in fact, we find no traces of a special stressing of this
preparatory activity. . . . Even in Justin's description the matter is
recounted simply and impersonally: bread is brought in, and wine and
water. No particular formalities are observed, no symbolism introduced
into the movement."[15] A number of observations are in order in
response to these comments. It is true that "in Justin's description the
matter is recounted simply and impersonally." The description is
contained in a single clause of fifteen words in Greek. The fact that his
description is so short and matter of fact is quite compatible with
a fully sacrificial understanding of the Eucharist, since the Offertory
would then be quite taken for granted. However, to say that "[n]o
particular formalities are observed, no symbolism introduced into the
movement," can not be so readily accepted. Saint Justin says that the
bread and wine are *prospheretai* to the president of the assembly. Now,
however this word is understood, it marks a development. The
Synoptic accounts speak of our Lord simply "taking (λαβὼν)" the
bread and wine, but here Saint Justin introduces the fact that someone
else gives the gifts to the president. Given what we know from the
Apostolic Tradition subsequently, it is probably already the deacons whom
Saint Justin mentions later. This, contrary to Jungmann's assertion,
is a particular formality that is a development from what is recorded in
the New Testament. And Saint Justin also tells us that this action takes
place after "we salute one another with a kiss." This has a clear
significance. It is the first mention of a detail from all the early liturgies,
that the Kiss of Peace preceded the Offertory, and the link with
Matthew 5:23–24 can hardly be doubted. "Therefore, if you are
offering your gift (προσφέρησ τὸ δῶρόν σου) at the altar, and there
remember that your brother has anything against you, leave your gift
at the altar, go and be reconciled with your brother first, and then come
and offer your gift." Here is an added reason for interpreting *prospheretai*
in its technical, sacrificial, sense, and it represents, contrary to
Jungmann's assertion, a clear "symbolism introduced into the movement."

We take it, therefore, that Jungmann's anti-sacrificial interpretation of Saint Justin does not stand up, and his down-playing of the Offertory is unjustified, and that Dix is correct on both counts. We saw earlier Pope Saint Clement's clearly sacrificial vision of the Eucharist, and it is not just in Rome that the Eucharist is understood in this way. According to Dix

> . . . every other local tradition . . . reveals the same understanding of the Eucharist as an "offering" (*prosphora*) or "sacrifice" (*thusia*)—something offered to God; and that the substance of the sacrifice is in every case in some sense the bread and the cup. . . . [T]here is no exception whatever anywhere in any Christian tradition in the second century and no hint of an alternative understanding of the rite anywhere.[16]

And his conclusion about the place of the Offertory on the basis of the early witness is as follows.

> Some "taking" of bread and wine before they could be blessed would seem a physical necessity in any Eucharistic rite. But such a mere necessary preparation for consecration is not at all the same thing as the offertory of the liturgical tradition, which is itself a ritual act with a significance of its own. It is an integral and original part of the whole Eucharistic action, not a preliminary to it, like the kiss of peace. This is not to say that its significance has always been sharply distinguished from that of what followed upon it. The offertory, the prayer and the communion are closely connected moments in a single continuous action, and each only finds its proper meaning as a part of the whole. Nevertheless, from before the end of the first century the offertory was understood to have a meaning of its own, without which the primitive significance of the whole Eucharist would be not only incomplete but actually destroyed.[17]

THE SUBSEQUENT HISTORY OF THE OFFERTORY

With Saint Justin, the "ritual act" of the Offertory appears for the first time. Whether or not that implies that there was no ritual act earlier we cannot say, but we have presented the case for concluding that it does not matter in any case. The place of the offertory in a sacrifice is essential from the very nature of sacrifice itself, and we have presented the evidence supporting the essential role of the people. However, it will be useful to review the history of the offertory to see if lessons can be learned about the importance of the rite in the Eucharist as a whole.

The basic idea in Saint Justin's account, which has remained constant ever since in East and West, is that it is the role of the deacons to bring the offerings to the bishop (or priest) at the altar. However, the aspect of the Offertory that is controverted and therefore of greater interest to our question is the role of the people, and it is dealt with explicitly for the first time in the *Apostolic Tradition*. A section of the document is a set of instructions about the catechumenate, the fundamental one being as follows: "Those to be baptized will bring nothing with them except what each one brings for the Eucharist. For it is fitting that those who are made worthy of doing so should provide the gifts on that same occasion."[18] There follows the order of service for Baptism, and it is explained that after they are baptized, they join for the first time in the Prayer of the Faithful and share the Sign of Peace. The Offertory is described as before and also the Eucharistic Prayer, and the section concludes: "These things we have handed over to you in brief concerning holy baptism and the holy offering (*prosphora*)."[19] The catechumens are to bring their offering for the Eucharist, and nothing else, since, in baptism, they are to be made worthy of offering for the first time. They are able to join for the first time in the Liturgy of the Eucharist, to be part of the Prayer of the Faithful and share the Sign of Peace, and to make the offering. This is understood to be the effect of Baptism. We would say that a newly baptized Christian is able to communicate for the first time. The original idea, on the other hand, was that the new Christian was able to "offer." The concluding sentence of the section implies that the Liturgy of the Eucharist was known quite simply as the "holy offering." Another piece of evidence from a later time, but completely coherent with the sense of the *Apostolic Tradition*, is the practice of Saint Ambrose in dealing with his catechumens. For Saint Ambrose, those newly baptized at the Easter Vigil had to wait until the Sunday after Easter, Low Sunday, before they could join in the Offertory procession and bring their gifts to the altar. The reason he gives is that this ceremony can only be performed by those who know its meaning and are fully initiated into the Church.[20] It is on the basis of evidence such as this that Dix concludes: "We know that all over Christendom the layman originally brought his *prosphora* of bread and wine with him to the *ecclesia;* that was the chief part of his 'liturgy.' We know, too that the deacons 'presented' these offerings upon the altar; that was a chief part of their 'liturgy.'"[21]

Not only is participation in the Offertory presented as the important new right of the newly baptized, it is also understood to be their duty. Jungmann says that "[b]y the time we reach Cyprian it has already become a general rule that the faithful should present gifts at the Eucharistic assembly."[22] Saint Cyprian chides a rich widow: "Would you come to the Sunday Eucharist without a sacrifice (*sacrificio*), and eat part of the sacrifice which a poor person has offered?"[23] One commentator sums up the situation: "He who did not offer was not thought to have joined in the bishop's or priest's sacrifice—the sacrifice which was also the faithful's. The axiom of the Jewish law: 'Thou shalt present thyself before me, not empty handed' (Exod. 23:15; Deut. 16:16) had the force of law to the Christian."[24]

Further evidence of the very great importance of the Offertory in the mind of the Church in these early centuries, is that, as the Church began to experience the need for discipline, that discipline was exercised in connection with the Offertory.

The whole rite was a true corporate offering by the Church in its hierarchical completeness of the Church in its organic unity, so much so that the penalty of mortal sin for members of every order was that they were forbidden to "offer," each according to the liturgy of his own order. The sinful layman was "forbidden to offer" (Cyprian, *Ep.* xvi. 14.), just as the unfrocked deacon was forbidden to "present," and the deposed bishop was forbidden to celebrate (*prospherein*) where we would have said "forbidden to receive Communion."[25]

The next point we find is that the penalty for serious offenses was exclusion precisely from the Offertory. The very first general councils of the Church, at Ancyra (314) and Nicaea (325), pass laws forbidding those guilty of serious misdemeanors from "offering" at the Eucharist. "The right to provide bread and wine was strictly reserved for those in full membership of the Church. Only those who had a right to communicate had also the right to offer; exclusion from communion meant exclusion from offering."[26] This essential nature of the Offertory is noted also by Jungmann: "Since the third century, then, it very quickly became a fixed rule that the faithful should offer their gifts at a common Eucharistic celebration, but because of the close connection with the performance of the sacred mystery it was from the very start recognised as a right restricted to those who were full members

of the Church, just like the reception of the Sacrament. . . . [and] the
gifts of all who openly lived in sin were to be refused. . . ."[27]

From the fourth century onward the Offertory developed differently in the East and in the West. In the East it became the custom
for the laity to bring their offerings to the sacristy or to a special
table in the church, the *prothesis,* before the service began. When the
Liturgy of the Word was over, the deacons fetched them from there to
bring them to the bishop at the altar. "This little ceremony soon
developed into one of the chief points of 'ritual splendour' in the Syrian-
Byzantine rites, and became the 'Great Entrance.'"[28] The Great
Entrance "is a climax of the Byzantine liturgy. Preceded by torches and
incense, the deacon and priest carry the host and the chalice, reverently
covered, from the *prothesis* through the nave of the church and back
into the sanctuary."[29] During this Great Entrance, the choir sings one
of the marvelous songs of the Eastern liturgy, the *Cherubikon,* and the
people prostrate in adoration. This developed liturgy of the Offertory
has remained constant in the East ever since.

In Gaul, the Offertory developed along the same lines as in
the East, and the people deposited the bread and wine in the sacristy
before the celebration began. The gifts were then carried to the altar in
solemn procession by the deacons and other ministers at the beginning
of the Liturgy of the Eucharist. "The gifts were carried in a receptacle
that was known as the 'tower,' from its shape, which was inspired
by the structure that covered the burial place of Christ in the basilica
of the Resurrection in Jerusalem. . . . The marks of veneration given
to the gifts suggest a procession of the Blessed Sacrament, down to
the words used in designating them, such as the 'mystery of the Lord's
body.'"[30] In the other churches of the West it was different.

> In the [rest of the] West the laity made their offerings for themselves at
> the chancel rail at the beginning of the Eucharist proper. Each man and
> woman came forward to lay their own offerings of bread in a linen cloth or
> a silver dish (called the *offertorium*) held by a deacon, and to pour their
> own flasks of wine into a great two-handled silver cup . . . held by another
> deacon. When the laity had made their offerings, each man for himself,
> the deacons bore them up and placed them on the altar.[31]

In these churches the bringing up of the gifts developed into the
Offertory Procession, accompanied by the Offertory Song. The bringing

up of the gifts in procession was understood to be in parallel with the Communion Procession. "Saint Augustine sees in this double procession an expression of the 'marvellous exchange' represented by the incarnation: Christ takes our humanity in order to bestow on us his divinity" (*Enarr. in ps. 129,* 7 [CCL 40: 1894–94; PL 37:1700–1]).[32] The conclusion of the Offertory rite was the Prayer over the Gifts (the *Secret*) said quietly by the priest.

This pattern remained constant in the churches of the West until the time of Charlemagne, when things began to change. Accompanying prayers were introduced, pronounced either by the faithful who bring their gift, or by the priest who receives it. An interesting example of such a prayer is the *Suscipe Sancte Pater* at the offering of the host, said by the priest in the Roman rite before the Second Vatican Council.

The first evidence that we have of this prayer occurs in a collection of private prayers that belonged to Charles the Bald. It recommends that he who is making the offering should say as he arrives at the altar: ". . . this spotless host, which *I* Thy unworthy servant, *offer* unto Thee. . . ." There developed gradually a profusion of prayers of recommendation, having the same function as the Secret. Some set out the intentions of the faithful who make the offering, others insist on the unworthiness of the sinner who is going to assist at the mystery, others again implore the suffrages of the saints or the benevolence of God.[33]

This ninth-century prayer marks the high point of active lay participation in the Eucharist, in either the East or the West. As well as processing with his gifts of bread and wine to the altar, the lay person also has a prayer to say expressing the intention of his offering. However, it was also at this time that the decline in the lay participation in the Offertory began, which led in the end to its almost complete disappearance from the Western liturgy. The gradual development of the Offertory in all the liturgies, which we have seen, fits perfectly with the interpretation being presented here. After the Constantinian Peace, when the Church was free to celebrate its ceremonies with a new exuberance, it makes perfect sense that the inherent meaning of the rite would come to more explicit liturgical expression. The development of the "ritual act" of the Offertory simply unfolds the meaning of what was always there implicitly. On the evidence we have reviewed thus far, the essential role of the Offertory is obvious, and its importance could not be more clearly highlighted. The heart of the Christian life was understood as "offering" the Holy Sacrifice, and that fundamental Christian duty was exercised by the whole Church, priest and people, precisely at the Offertory of the Mass. It was precisely at this moment, however, that the change took place in the fortune of the Offertory in the Latin Church which has provided the second prong of the argument against its essential role.

THE DECLINE OF THE OFFERTORY IN THE WEST

Different factors can be pointed to as probably contributing to the decline of the Offertory in the West. One is the gradual introduction of the use of unleavened bread in the Eucharist. The custom began to appear in the West in the ninth century and had become general by the eleventh. Its implication for the Offertory was that the people could no longer bring their own bread from home to offer at Mass, as they had done before. A second factor was the emergence of the private Mass. The introduction in the eleventh century of the "complete missal," in which all the texts of the songs, readings, and prayers were given in the order in which they were to be used during Mass, meant that Mass could now be celebrated by a priest with only a few people, or even with only a server. Monasticism was of enormous influence during these centuries, and in the monasteries, as more and more monks were ordained, the private Mass became common. The fact that the liturgy continued to be celebrated in Latin which was not understood by the common people was a factor in distancing the people from the priest at the altar.

To these causes must be added the monastic and canonical character that the liturgy had gradually acquired. Chanting became an increasingly complex matter and therefore the prerogative of canons, trained bodies of singers, and cantors, as the choir replaced the congregation. This element of substitution was aggravated in cathedrals and abbeys by the installation of roodscreens, which, from the fourteenth century on, often became more or less opaque partitions between the faithful and the few individuals who were the sole agents in the Eucharistic celebration. All these factors turned the laity into onlookers so passive that the liturgical books no longer even mentioned their presence.[34]

Although the active participation of the people ceased little by little, the prayers that had served as a commentary on them were preserved. "Their preservation perpetuated the idea underlying the rites that had disappeared. From now on, everything, both words and actions, was confined to the priest and his ministers at the altar; as for the faithful, they still united themselves in spirit to all these ceremonies, which still represent today, after so many centuries, their active participation of former times."[35] Jungmann reports an interesting vignette highlighting the oddness of these developments. "A very festive rite of offertory procession [was] still in use at the solemn papal Mass for a canonisation. . . . However, the general attitude of the later Roman liturgy towards the offertory procession, the attitude of reserve and even avoidance, [. . .] led to the very singular result that the celebrant as a rule [took] no notice of the procession even when it still occur[red]."[36]

The Offertory of the Roman rite reached its lowest point in the Missal of Pius V of 1570, which remained the norm until the renewal after the Second Vatican Council. The rubrics of the Offertory were as follows: "After the Prayer over the Gifts, if it is a solemn Mass, the Deacon hands the Celebrant the paten with the Host: if private, the Priest himself takes the paten with the Host. . . . The Deacon puts the wine, the subdeacon the water in the chalice: or if it is a private Mass, the Priest pours both." We have thereby come full circle and returned to the simplest form of the Offertory as described in the *Apostolic Tradition,* with only the deacon having any active role apart from the priest. All that has changed quite considerably in the new Mass of Paul VI, but we will leave a consideration of those changes until later.

On the basis of this change in the Western liturgy, it is argued that since the Offertory declined in this dramatic fashion it cannot be essential to the Eucharist. Now, what disappeared in the West was the active participation of the laity in the Offertory. From this it does indeed follow that the active participation of the laity in the rite of the Offertory is not essential, that a "ritual act" of offering can be missing. But does this absence of a "ritual act" imply that there is no Offertory by the laity? One fact makes it clear that it does not. There has never been any active participation by the laity in the ritual of the Offertory in the East. There, the laity brought their gifts to the sacristy, and the deacons carried the gifts from there to the altar in the magnificent procession of the Great Entrance. And yet there has never been any doubt that this Great Entrance was giving ritual expression to the offering of the people. The gifts belong to the people, who brought them to the sacristy, and the deacons were carrying them to the altar on the people's behalf. So, a "ritual act" is not necessary to constitute the Offertory. The important question is: To whom do the gifts belong? Are they the individual property of the priest which he is offering on his own behalf, or is he offering them on behalf of the Church as a whole?

That the gifts are the property of the people is not in dispute. Clark himself admits as much when he concedes, albeit grudgingly, that the people did have a role to play in providing the bread and wine for the sacrifice. He continues:

> It is altogether another and more difficult question as to whether it was the custom and duty of the faithful *to provide* the Eucharistic elements. It is true that in due course the provision of the bread and wine took on the *signification* of the participation of the faithful in the sacrifice at which they were assisting, and hence opened the way for a *ritual* presentation of the elements as being a more effective way of symbolising that participation; but the faithful obviously participated in the offering of the Mass *prior* to the introduction of a ritual presentation. It is therefore quite clear that the ritual presentation of the gifts, even the express provision of those gifts by the people, does not belong to the essential Offertory rite.[3] . . . In fact there is not the slightest doubt that the actual provision of the elements by all the people present did not enter into the primitive Eucharist as an essential factor in its constitution. It was not the bread and wine that had sacrificial value, but the Body and Blood of Christ. So far as evidence is available, there is nothing to suggest that this provision of the elements is something *special*, separate from the general provision of charity.[38]

Clark's question is as to the significance of the provision of the gifts. On his understanding of a sacrifice, the provision of the gifts can be of no significance whatever. On the understanding of sacrifice being presented here, the provision of the gifts is all that matters, for the one who provides the gifts is the one who is offering the sacrifice, and this perspective is corroborated by the institution of the Mass Offering.

The theology of the Mass Offering has not always been well understood. It has often been considered as a stipend offered for the sustenance of the priest who offers the Mass, and that is clearly part of its meaning, as it was part of the original Offertory. The other interpretation understands the Mass Offering precisely as a participation in the Offertory of the Mass, and that interpretation has now been formally accepted as the teaching of the Church. Pope Paul VI decided the issue in *Firma in Traditione* (1974).

> It is a long-established tradition in the Church that the faithful, desiring in a religious and ecclesial spirit to participate more intimately in the Eucharistic Sacrifice, add to it a form of sacrifice of their own by which they contribute in a particular way to the needs of the Church and especially to the sustenance of its ministers (1 Tim. 5:18, 1 Cor. 9:7–14). This practice by which the faithful unite themselves more closely with Christ offering himself as a victim, thus deriving more abundant fruit from the sacrifice, has not merely been approved but has been positively encouraged by the Church. It is a sign of the union of the baptised person with Christ and of the faithful with the priest who exercises his ministry for their good.[39]

This interpretation of the Mass Offering clinches the issue. It is clear that the priest is making the offering on behalf of the people. Every Mass that is offered is, in principle, open to being offered for an Offering, and therefore it is clear that the gifts offered are not the property of the priest. They belong to the Church in general, or to the individual on whose behalf the Mass is being offered. It follows that, despite there being no active participation of the laity in the "ritual act" of the Offertory, despite the fact that the laity may not be present at all at a private Mass, the fact remains that the gifts are offered on their behalf, and the original meaning of the Offertory remains intact, although in a highly atrophied and inadequate form, and this second argument of Suarez and Clark must fall.

The Reform of the Offertory after Vatican II

To complete this discussion on the role of the Offertory in the Liturgy of the Eucharist, there is interesting evidence to be brought forward

surrounding the reform of the Offertory rite of the Mass during
the recent post-conciliar liturgical reform. Given the dominant opinion
among liturgical scholars that the Offertory does not belong to the
sacrifice of the Eucharist, it was inevitable that the effort would be
made to reform the rite to remove any ambiguities in this regard. The
Mass of Pope Pius V, in use prior to the reform, had an Offertory
rite that was markedly sacrificial. The actual rite itself was simple, as
we have observed already, and the people had no active part, but the
prayers spoke repeatedly and insistently in sacrificial terms. At the
Offertory, the rubrics specified that the priest should raise the paten
with the bread and pray:

> Receive, O holy Father, almighty and eternal God, this spotless host which
> I, your unworthy servant, offer to you, my living and true God, for my own
> countless sins, offences, and negligences; and for all present here, as well
> as for all faithful Christians both living and dead, that it may profit me and
> them as a means of reaching salvation in the eternal life. Amen.

When he raised the chalice he was to pray:

> We offer to you, O Lord, the chalice of salvation, humbly begging your
> mercy that it may arise before your divine majesty as a pleasing fragrance
> for our salvation and for that of the whole world. Amen.

There then followed the *Orate fratres*: "Pray brethren, that my sacrifice
and yours may be acceptable to God the Almighty Father." As one
commentator has recently observed:

> The most striking thing about these prayers is the way they anticipate the
> Eucharistic Prayer that is to follow. Thus, even though it is simply bread
> and wine that lie on the altar at this point, the prayers speak of "this spotless
> host (victim)" and "the chalice of salvation. . . . "[40]

This is what had been causing difficulty for the scholars of the liturgy
since the change in opinion about the Offertory at the beginning of
the twentieth century. What the liturgy was saying did not fit with the
current understanding of the Eucharist, and the dominant view was
that the Offertory should be radically changed, if not removed completely.
Inevitably, then, "from the beginning of the reform the existing
offertory rite was seen as especially problematical." The effort would
be made to remove "any excess in the rite that . . . is proleptic in

relation to the anaphora . . . and thus makes the presentation of the gifts an offering and an end, even a sacrifice, in itself. . . ."[41]

The initial project of the Consilium for the Reform of the Liturgy, *The Project of 1964: Specimen provisorium*, was a radical one.

> The priest's reception of the gifts from the people is mentioned but is not described. . . . [Then], [s]tanding at the centre of the altar, the priest first receives and then reverently holds the cup in his right hand and the vessel or plate with bread in his left (without any further or explicit gesture of offering). Before placing the vessels ceremonially upon the altar, he says a single formula: "As this bread was scattered over the mountains and was gathered into one and as wine from many vines flowed into one, so may your Church be gathered from the ends of the earth into your kingdom. Glory to you for ever." [And] . . . the invitation *Orate, fratres* and its response are omitted.[42]

The notable thing about this proposal is that all the language of "offering" is removed from the rite, and this was in accordance with the deliberate intention of the drafters.

> We must therefore remove or change elements that suggest any kind of offering of Christ's body and blood in this rite and that anticipate expressions belonging exclusively to the canon of the Mass.[43]

Certain changes were introduced in the first *Missa normativa* of 1965, but the thrust of the project remained the same. "With regard to the texts, the intent was to remove anything referring to the offering of the body and blood of Christ, while changing the *elevatio* of the gifts into a solemn *depositio*."[44] Presumably, the removal of the elevation of the gifts was to avoid even the impression of "offering" that this gesture could imply.

This revised Order of Mass was celebrated during the meeting of the Synod of Bishops of 1967, and Pope Paul VI participated in three of them. The Pope and the bishops then made recommendations that were to be taken into account in the further development of the new rite. Pope Paul's reactions are of considerable interest, in the light of our discussion, for he clearly did not share the received wisdom of liturgical scholarship about the Offertory.

> The offertory seems lacking, because the faithful are not allowed any part in it (even though it should be the part of the Mass in which their activity

is more direct and obvious). . . . The offertory should be given a special prominence so that the faithful (or their representatives) may exercise their special role as offerers.[45]

Subsequently the Pope expressed his mind on the new Mass formula in a document known as "The Pope's Wishes." Part of what he called for concerned the Offertory. "There should be a single set of formulas that will express the idea of an offering of human toil in union with the sacrifice of Christ. There should also be active participation of the congregation. . . ."[46] In the next schema of March 1968, changes were introduced in response to this intervention of Pope Paul VI . The two formulas for the bread and cup were composed according to his wish. "On the other hand, every misconception is to be avoided: it is not a sacrifice of bread and wine or an offering of the body and blood of Christ or a consecratory epiclesis."[47] In the new formulas there was still no mention of "offering." Bugnini reports Pope Paul's response.

> The Pope noted that the formulas used in offering the bread and the wine "are two fine euchological utterances, but they do not express any intention of offering if the phrase 'which we offer to you' is removed from the two formulas; without it they are not offering formulas. The phrase seems to be what gives the gesture and words their specific meaning as offering. However I leave the decision to the collegial judgment of the Consilium."[48]

According to Bugnini, there were 12 for retention, 14 against, and 5 for "finding an expression that would refer to the presentation of the elements for the sacrifice, but without using the term 'offer.'"[49] Bugnini does not explain how the decision was made in the light of this voting, but, as we know, the difficult phrase "which we offer to you" was retained in the Offertory formulas of the May 1968 schema and in the definitive text of 1969. McManus concludes his account of the process with one last piece of information.

> With the promulgation of the *Order of Mass* in 1969, the five-year process was completed. It remains only to note one change from the May 1968 schema. . . . It is the restoration of the invitation *Orate, fratres* and full response before the prayer over the gifts from the 1570 Order of Mass.[50]

So, what was the outcome of the reform process? The dominant school of liturgical opinion had set out to remove all semblance of "offering" from the Offertory, but the effort was not successful. If one compares the prayers of the new rite with that of 1570, the substance is identical. In both cases the bread and wine are "offered" to God. The language of 1969 is less overtly sacrificial, but is, if anything, more deeply so, since the meaning of sacrifice, the human cooperation with the sacrifice of Christ that Pope Paul VI spoke of, is brought out in these beautiful new prayers. The *Orate fratres* has remained. The only significant change from 1570 to 1969 is that the active participation of the people, which had faded out in the early Middle Ages, has once again been restored. The process also revealed the mind of Pope Paul VI in the matter. It is clear that he understood the Offertory as an Offertory, and he was insistent that the faithful should be actively involved, so that they "may exercise their special role as offerers." It is probably not without significance that Pope Paul VI had been Archbishop of Milan, since the Ambrosian rite always retained the people's Offertory in the form of a presentation of the gifts by a group of representatives of the congregation.

It is appropriate to complete this story by presenting as a commentary the understanding of the Offertory taught by Pope John Paul II in his document on the Eucharist, *Dominicae cenae* (1980).

> Although all those who participate in the Eucharist do not confect the sacrifice as he does, they offer with him, by virtue of the common priesthood, their own *spiritual sacrifices* represented by the bread and wine from the moment of their presentation at the altar. For this liturgical action, which takes a solemn form in almost all liturgies, has a "spiritual value and meaning." The bread and wine become in a sense a symbol of all that the Eucharistic assembly brings, on its own part, as an offering to God and offers spiritually.

It is important that this first moment of the Liturgy of the Eucharist in the strict sense should find expression in the attitude of the participants. There is a link between this and the Offertory "procession" provided for in the recent liturgical reform and accompanied, in keeping with ancient tradition, by a psalm or song. A certain length of time must be allowed so that all can become aware of this act, which is given expression at the same time by the words of the celebrant.[51]

The Pope's teaching is not ambiguous. He implicitly rejects the argument that would denigrate the Offertory on the grounds of its simple form in the Roman liturgy when he notes that it "takes

a solemn form in almost all liturgies." He gives it a full sacrificial interpretation when he observes that in it the people exercise their common priesthood and "offer . . . their own *spiritual sacrifices* represented
by the bread and wine from the moment of their presentation at the
altar. . . . The bread and wine become in a sense a symbol of all that
the Eucharistic assembly brings on its own part, as an offering to
God and offers spiritually." And he affirms explicitly the point that this
whole argument has been trying to establish, that the Offertory is "the
first moment of the Liturgy of the Eucharist in the strict sense."

CONCLUSION

And so we return to where we began this chapter and examine again
Gregory Dix's description of the "ideal" Eucharist. For him, the
Eucharist has four parts: the Offertory, the Eucharistic Prayer, the
Fraction, and Communion. Now, having recalled from a survey of
liturgical history the great importance of the Offertory "in almost all
liturgies," and countered the arguments used to set it aside as a merely
preparatory rite, the obvious conclusion mentioned already is there
to be drawn, that the Eucharist is not a one-act rite focused in the
Eucharistic Prayer, but that it conforms to the simple three-part structure of a communion sacrifice: the offertory, the priestly mediation,
and the meal.

---

1. Coppens, *"L'Offrande des fidèles dans la Liturgie eucharistique ancienne,"* 108.

2. SC 248, 192.

3. Helmut Moll, *Die Lehre von der Eucharistie als Opfer: Eine dogmengeschichtliche
Untersuchung vom Neuen Testament bis Irenäus von Lyon* (Köln-Bonn: Peter
Hanstein Verlag, 1975), 110.

4. Ibid., 115.

5. Ludwig Schopp, editor, *The Fathers of the Church, A New Translation,*
Volume 1 (Washington: The Catholic University of America Press, 1947),
41–42.

6. Jean Colson, *Les fonctions ecclésiales aux deux premiers siècles* (Paris: Desclée
de Brouwer, 1956), 211.

7. Coppens's position is less developed but no less emphatic: "The writings of Saint Justin . . . witness even much less [than earlier Fathers] the use of a food offering." Coppens, *"L'Offrande des fidèles dans la Liturgie eucharistique ancienne,"* 111.

8. Joseph A. Jungmann, sj, *The Mass of the Roman Rite: Its Origins and Development,* vol. 1 (New York: Benziger Brothers, 1950), 26.

9. Ibid.

10. Justin, *Apology 1,* 65 (PG Vl, 428).

11. Dix, *The Shape of the Liturgy,* 110.

12. Robert J. Daly, *Christian Sacrifice: The Judaeo-Christian Background before Origen* (Washington: The Catholic University of America Press, 1978), 325.

13. Moll, *Die Lehre von der Euchariste als Opfer,* 125, n. 16.

14. Jungmann, *The Mass of the Roman Rite,* vol. 1, 26–27.

15. Jungmann, *The Mass of the Roman Rite,* vol. 2, 1.

16. Dix, *The Shape of the Liturgy,* 112–113.

17. Dix, *The Shape of the Liturgy,* 110.

18. *Trad. Ap.* 20, SC 11bis, 80.

19. *Trad. Ap.* 21, SC 11bis, 94.

20. Ambrose, *In Ps. 118 Expos.,* Prologue, 2 (PL 15.1198–1199).

21. Dix, *The Shape of the Liturgy,* 120.

22. Jungmann, *The Mass of the Roman Rite,* vol. 2, 2.

23. *De opere et eleemosynas,* 15, CSEL 3, 1, 384.21–23.

24. A. Croegart, *The Mass: A Liturgical Commentary; Volume II, The Mass of the Faithful* (London: Burns & Oates, 1959), 74.

25. Dix, 117.

26. Clifford Howell, "Reforming the Liturgy: The Offertory," *Clergy Review,* LII, No. 6, June 1967, 468.

27. Jungmann, *The Mass of the Roman Rite,* vol. 2, 19f.

28. Dix, *The Shape of the Liturgy,* 120.

29. Jungmann, *The Mass of the Roman Rite,* vol. 2, 5.

30. Robert Cabié, *The Church at Prayer, Volume 2: The Eucharist* (Collegeville: The Liturgical Press, 1986), 78–79.

31. Dix, *The Shape of the Liturgy*, 120.

32. Cabié, *The Church at Prayer*, vol. 2, 78.

33. Dom Bernard Capelle, OSB, *A New Light on the Mass*, 2 ed., (Dublin/ London: Clonmore and Reynolds, Ltd./Burns Oates & Washbourne, 1961), 25.

34. Cabié, *The Church at Prayer*, vol. 2, 139.

35. Capelle, *A New Light on the Mass*, 26.

36. Jungmann, *The Mass of the Roman Rite*, vol. 2, 19. (The fact that Jungmann's book was written prior to the renewal of the liturgy after the Second Vatican Council required the altering of the tenses of his report.)

37. Alan Clark, *The Function of the Offertory Rite in the Mass*, 327. (Emphasis in the original.)

38. Ibid., 329.

39. AAS 66 (1974) 308.

40. Cabié, *The Church at Prayer*, vol. 2, 163.

41. Frederick R. McManus, "The Roman Order of Mass from 1964 to 1969: The Preparation of the Gifts," in *Shaping English Liturgy*, eds. Peter C. Finn, James M. Schellman (Washington: The Pastoral Press, 1990), 107–138, at 111.

42. Ibid., 120–22.

43. The Consilium, Study Section 10, *De Ordine Missae, Schemata, no. 39, De Missali*, 30 Sept. 1964, *Report on the Prayer over the Gifts*, no. 57.

44. McManus, "The Order of Mass, 1964–1969," 124.

45. Annibale Bugnini, *The Reform of the Liturgy 1948–1975* (Collegeville: The Liturgical Press, 1990), 364.

46. Ibid., 369.

47. McManus, "The Order of Mass, 1964–1969," 127.

48. Bugnini, *The Reform of the Liturgy 1948–1975*, 379.

49. Ibid.

50. McManus, "The Order of Mass, 1964–1969," 129.

51. AAS 72 (1980), 131 (English translation from Austin Flannery, OP, ed, *More Postconciliar Documents* [New York and Dublin: Costello Publishing Company and Dominican Publications, § 9, 75.])

Chapter 5

The Meal Theory of Sacrifice

We have presented the three-part structure of Old Testament sacrifice, that the communion sacrifice of Israel consisted of an offertory, the priestly mediation, and the meal. We have presented the case in favor of identifying it fundamentally with the three-part structure of the Eucharist. If this alternative concept of sacrifice is to be acceptable it must also fit with the Sacrifice of the Cross. And so it will be necessary to proceed to the examination of the Sacrifice of the Cross in the light of the structure of Old Testament sacrifice. So far, in applying the notion to the Eucharist, it has been sufficient to focus on the general structure of sacrifice, and on the communion sacrifice in particular. When we come to consider the Cross, the notion of sacrifice needs to be both widened and deepened in different directions. It will no longer be sufficient to focus on the communion sacrifice since the Cross is the fulfilment of all the sacrifices of Israel, and we will, therefore, be required to examine the different forms of sacrifice more in detail. Also, since the Eucharist is clearly in the form of a cereal offering, the structure could be observed in its simplest outline. This, obviously, does not apply to the Sacrifice of the Cross, which is clearly patterned on an animal sacrifice, where the victim is a living being. A first, and crucial, point to be established will be the significance of the death of the animal within the structure of a sacrifice. It will no longer be sufficient to observe the structure of sacrifice simply on the surface of its separate parts; an overall interpretation of the structure needs to be established in order to decide how the different parts are related to each other. Then and only then will it be possible to decide where the death fits in, and what role it plays in the overall process.

For this purpose we will be basing ourselves on one of the standard interpretations, the meal theory of sacrifice. It is not new, and was well elaborated as long ago as the first half of the thirteenth century by William of Auvergne, Bishop of Paris, and taken up again to some extent by Maurice de la Taille in his works on the Eucharist, but failed to find general acceptance.[1] Since the end of the nineteenth century, it has come to be widely accepted among scholars of comparative religion, but, when applied to the Old Testament, continues to be rejected almost unanimously by exegetes and theologians.[2] However, it is the only theory that fits with the three-part structure of sacrifice which has been espoused here, and so a summary presentation of its general features must be made.

THE MEAL THEORY OF SACRIFICE[3]

The basic understanding of sacrifice in the Catholic tradition as a gift offered to God is obviously correct. However, an examination of the Old Testament evidence makes it clear that the definition is too broad, for not any gift has place in the liturgy of sacrifice. The only offerings permissible for sacrifice were the staple articles of daily food: oxen, sheep, goats, pigeons, and of field produce, grain and oil and wine. The ass, the horse, gold, jewels, and clothing were more highly treasured possessions, but were not permissible offerings for sacrifice. What is offered in sacrifice is called food or bread, *lehem*, destined for God (Leviticus 3:11, 16; 21:6, 8, 17, 22; 22:25; Numbers 28:2, 24; Ezra 44:7; Malachi 1:7) Furthermore, sacrifices are never offered to God raw, but must be prepared. After being killed, the animal is skinned and then cut into pieces. In the case of cereals, they are offered as flour, the olives as oil, flour and oil can be offered to God as bread; grapes are offered in the form of wine, and the cereal offering must be further prepared by pouring oil on it or adding incense. The meat for a communion sacrifice, destined for the priests and the offerer after it has been offered to God and returned for the participants, is then cooked in water. With this in mind, the utensils of the temple are all culinary instruments (Exodus 25:29). The altar is called the "Table of the Lord" (Malachi 1:7, 12), and the word for arranging the different pieces of meat on the altar, *arak*, is the same as that used for laying a table (Leviticus 1:8 and Isaiah 21:5). This understanding of the altar is to be found also in the New Testament. Speaking of Jewish sacrifice, Saint Paul says, "are not those who eat the sacrifices participants in the altar?" (1 Corinthians

10:18), and then, making the comparison with the Christian sacrifice, he says, "You cannot partake of the table of the Lord and of the table of demons" (1 Corinthians 10:21), clearly understanding "altar" and "table" as synonymous. In Hebrews 13:10 we are told that "We have an altar from which those who serve the tabernacle have no right to eat," making it clear that an altar is something from which one "eats."

This is surely an impressive array of evidence, and it can hardly be denied that a meal has some role to play in sacrifice. The stumbling block is the idea implied by the full meal theory that God is understood to "eat" the food which is offered to Him. This is the aspect of the meal theory that is generally rejected by Christian interpreters. It is argued that, while the theory may explain sacrifice in other religions, it cannot apply to Old Testament sacrifice since it implies a notion of God that is completely alien to the Bible.[4] The argument is that any evidence in favor of interpreting a sacrifice as a meal is the survival of primitive ideas persisting in Israelite religion, but totally incompatible with Israel's high idea of God, to be found in texts like Psalm 50:13, which mocks the idea that God could be fed by his people: "Do I eat the flesh of bulls or drink the blood of goats?" The issue has two nuances, depending on whether one looks at it from the side of God or from the side of the people. On the one hand, does it make sense to understand God as "eating" the food that is laid before Him, and on the other hand, can one possibly conceive of the people as "feeding" God?

The issue involved in the first question hangs on the interpretation of the holocaust or burnt offering, where the food items are burned on the altar. Now, if one rejects the meal theory, one reverts to some version or other of the one-act theory of sacrifice which understands sacrifice simply as a gift offered to God, with no suggestion of any ulterior purpose such as God's "eating" it. The penal substitution theory of sacrifice understands the burning as the altar fire destroying a sin-bearing victim, symbolically purifying the offerer from his sin. But this interpretation is ruled out since the burning forms part of the communion sacrifice as well as the sin offering. The burning of the gift can also be understood as the offerer destroying his gift, thus signifying his total handing over of his property, taking it out of his sphere of use completely. There is no doubt that this is indeed an important aspect of the gesture of burning. The gift in kind is an expression of the gift of self, and the destruction can be understood reasonably as symbolic of the totality of the gift. This is surely part of the meaning of the holocaust, or whole burnt offering, where the gift is burnt in its totality. But does it explain all the aspects of the liturgy of the holocaust? There is the fact that the food items must be prepared as for cooking before being handed over to the priest to be burned on the altar. What would be the sense of that if the point of the burning was simply destruction? The Bible's understanding of the burning is also important, and on this point let us listen to Gayford.

> The "portion of the Lord" was conveyed to Him by being burnt in the fire of the altar. The technical word for this action is again full of significance. This word, *hiqtir,* means literally "to cause to go up in sweet smoke"; so this altar-burning is "for a sweet savour unto the Lord" (Lev. 4:31). The verb and its kindred noun *qetoreth* (sweet smoke) are used *only* of sacrificial burning and sacrificial smoke (which includes the smoke of incense). It is evidently meant that the effect of the sacrificial fire upon the Offering was to refine and etherialize what is carnal and earthly; the gross flesh, changed into the sweet smoke, ascends heavenwards, until it reaches the heavenly realms. It is significant also that while *hiqtir* is used only in sacrificial language, the word *saraph* (= "to burn up"), the ordinary secular word for *destructive* burning, is never used of the portions burnt upon the altar . . . [but only of burning in] a fire lit "without the camp," their skins, etc. (Lev. 4:12).[5]

Now, if this burning is not destructive, it is easy to interpret it as God "consuming" the portion of food that has been set aside for Him on the altar. The fire first came down and "consumed the holocaust" in Aaron's first sacrifice (Leviticus 9:24: the word "consume" is the straightforward word *tachal* meaning "to eat"). The same happened for Gideon (Judges 6:21), for Elijah (1 Kings 18:38), and for Solomon (2 Chronicles 7:1). In each case the fire "ate" the sacrifice. Of these episodes the most instructive for our purposes is the meeting of the Lord with Gideon. After the Lord had commissioned Gideon, the encounter proceeds as follows.

> Gideon said to him, "If I have found favour in your sight, give me a sign that it is you who speak to me. I beg you, do not go away until I come back, I will bring you my offering (*minhah, thusia*) and set it down before you." And he answered, "I will stay until you return." Gideon went away and prepared a young goat and made unleavened cakes with an ephah of flour. He put the meat into a basket and the broth in a pot, then brought

it all to him under the terebinth. As he came near, the angel of the Lord said to him, "Take the meat and unleavened cakes, put them on this rock and pour the broth over them." Gideon did so. Then the angel of the Lord reached out the tip of the staff in his hand and touched the meat and unleavened cakes. Fire sprang from the rock and consumed ["ate"] the meat and unleavened cakes, and the angel of the Lord vanished before his eyes. Then Gideon knew this was the angel of the Lord, and he said, "Alas, my Lord! I have seen the angel of the Lord face to face!" The Lord answered him, "Peace be with you; have no fear; you will not die." Gideon built an altar there to the Lord and called it The-Lord-is-Peace. (Judges 6:17–24)

This text gives a commentary on the meaning of sacrifice. Gideon's offering is a *minhah,* the word which became the technical word for a communion sacrifice of bread and wine, and he built an altar in memory of the occasion. Gideon was treating the Lord as an honored guest, and the sign of God's favor was that He "ate" the food set before Him. It is the same word that is used of the fire on the altar that "eats" the holocaust in Leviticus 6:3, and again of Aaron and his sons "eating" their portion of a cereal offering in Leviticus 6:9. Surely, in the light of these texts, the symbolic understanding of God "eating" the food that is laid before Him cannot be simply ruled out of court as gross and unworthy of a genuine biblical idea of God.

What then of the idea that would understand what is happening as Israel "feeding" God, for this is Eichrodt's formulation? There is no doubt that such a notion would be completely alien to the Bible. The suggestion that God could be dependent on His people for His very existence, even symbolically, cannot possibly be entertained. But this is not at all what is involved. One clear indication is that not all kinds of food were offered in the sacrifices. Wild game, wild birds, fish, and the natural produce of the land that grew wild, such as wild fruit, milk, and honey, were not admitted. Animal offerings must be "of the herd and of the flocks" (Exodus 22:29, 30; Leviticus 1:2), and the vegetable offerings only those cultivated by the people themselves, grain and oil and wine. In other words, the offerings must be "the work of human hands." If "feeding" was all that was involved, what difference would it make what sort of food was offered? Surely, it is clearly not just food that is in question for the "feeding" of God, but food as an expression of the life of the people themselves, which they are offering to God as an expression of a sharing of life with Him.

Furthermore, it is clear from the ritual of sacrifice that it is based on a spiritual understanding of the meal. A meal is not only a matter of nourishment of the body, but is also, and from the human point of view more importantly, a matter of table fellowship that establishes unity and kinship. The proper analogy for the place attributed to God in Israelite sacrifice is not "feeding," which is reserved for animals and infants, but the treatment of an honored guest at a meal, and the etiquette of the table constitutes a complex form of communication which far transcends the simple function of nourishment.

> By the etiquette of the table, one can express the importance of the guest by the type of hospitality offered, his place at the table, when he is served, and by the nature and quality of the food one offers him. . . . Now, what the etiquette of the table is to an ordinary meal, the ritual is to the sacrificial meal.[6]

Consider the story in Genesis 18, where "The Lord appeared to Abraham by the terebinth of Mamre" (18:1). Abraham saw three men and he entertained them as his guests. As the story unfolds it becomes clear that one of the three men is the Lord Himself, and part of the meaning of the story is God's condescending to come down and accept Abraham's hospitality as his friend. Consider again the visit of the angel of the Lord to Manoah in Judges 13. "Then Manoah said to the angel of the Lord, 'Can we persuade you to stay, while we prepare a kid for you?' But the angel of the Lord answered Manoah, 'Although you press me, I will not partake of your food. But if you will, you may offer a holocaust to the Lord'" (13:15–16). As Marx comments on this: "Judges 13:15–19 shows clearly the continuity between an ordinary meal and a sacrifice: what was originally meant as a meal for a visitor can just as well be used as a holocaust."[7] This is the context of the biblical ritual of sacrifice. God is not understood as coming to the meal to be fed, but His coming is seen as an act of deep condescension, accepting the invitation of His people to share in their meal as a sign of His willingness to share their life. By variations in the type of sacrifice, the nature of the food items involved, their manner of preparation, the distribution of the parts among the various participants, the moment and the place of their consumption, the ritual is able to express how the people understand and live their relationship with God in ways that cannot be put into words. For instance, the item of food habitually apportioned to God, a small animal, corresponds to what would normally be offered to a guest (see, for example, Judges 13:15; 2 Samuel 12:4). And the flour required for a cereal offering had to be the finest wheat flour obtainable. It was not used for ordinary purposes except by those who were known for luxurious living; it was reserved for honored guests (Genesis 18:6). The different types of sacrifice reproduce the two forms of Israelite hospitality. The pattern of Genesis 18:1–8 and 1 Samuel 28:21–25, where the meal is placed before the guest and the host does not take part, corresponds to the holocaust and the vegetable offering in which only God and the priests participate. The more normal type of hospitality, as in 1 Samuel 9:22–24, where the guest is invited by his host to sit at table and take the place of honor, corresponds to the communion sacrifice, in which God is honoured by being served first and being given the better part, the fat (see Genesis 45:18; Deuteronomy 32:14; Ezra 24:3; Psalm 81:17). The whole sacrificial system of Israel is full of such parallels with table etiquette, and can surely be seen as an elaborate statement of Israel's relationship with God. In offering a meal to God, Israel manifests the people's belief in the Lord as a living being, a person. Like them, He eats food and takes pleasure in a meal, thus revealing Himself as One with whom one can communicate.

> In bringing Him dishes prepared from the produce of their land, Israel expresses her conviction that God belongs to the community of the sons of Israel and is bound to their land. He is the invisible guest . . . at all the festivals which express the joy of His people. He dwells among them like a king in his palace and is honoured as such every day. By means of sacrifice, the Lord thus appears as a God who is close, familiar, accessible at every moment, a God whom every Israelite, whatever his social condition, has the privilege of receiving as his guest. By sharing a meal with men, God establishes with them the closest possible relationship, that created by table fellowship.[8]

One last point remains to be considered in regard to the general notion of a sacrifice as a sacred meal shared with God. We have presented the evidence in favor of the idea that a meal forms part of a sacrifice, and that God is to be considered as a participant in this meal. But just how important is the meal? The one-act theory of sacrifice puts all the emphasis on the offering, and, if a meal were to be considered as belonging to the sacrifice, it could only be understood as coming after the important core of the sacrifice, the offering. It could then be taken as an expression of God's acceptance of the offering, for example, but it would still be understood in terms of the offering, which is always understood as the truly important action of the sacrifice. Does an interpretation along such lines do justice to the evidence? So far, we have considered the overall three-part structure common to all three, and the basic concept that unites them, the meal, and now we must see if we can discern the pattern that makes them a coherent set. In approaching this issue, it is necessary now to examine the three sacrifices of Israel, the sin offering, the holocaust, and the communion sacrifice, in their differences and inter-relationship.

THE THREE SACRIFICES OF ISRAEL

The offertory is common to all the sacrifices. This could mean that it is the fundamental and most important action of a sacrifice, or it could mean rather that it should be understood as a necessary condition for the unfolding of the acts that follow. However, the one-act theory of sacrifice is not tempted to see the ultimate significance here, in the action of the offerer of the sacrifice, since its whole focus is on the action of the priest. Now, the two acts of the priestly mediation are basically the same in all three sacrifices: the ceremonial use of the blood and the sharing out of the food, offering His portion to God and burning it on the altar. Could this be where greatest significance is to be discerned? Notice that in the one-act theory of sacrifice, the offerer is effectively ignored and these first two parts of the structure are conflated into a single priestly "offering" of the sacrifice. The actual ritual of sacrifice, however, makes clear that this is a mistake. The "offering" of the sacrifice is not the action of one alone, for the offerer and the priest both "offer" the gift. The word used for the action of the offerer is *hiqrib* (Leviticus 1:3, "to bring near"). The same word is used of the priest's work in presenting the blood (1:5) and the flesh (1:13) on the altar. So, the offerer first offers the gift to God into the hands of the priest, and the priest then offers it to God by placing it on the altar. The most important point here is that "offering" in the sense that we normally mean the word, of giving a gift to God, is the action of the offerer, not the priest. The gift is the work of his hands, of his herd and his flock: It is his sacrifice, not the priest's. The priest is performing a mediating role between the offerer and God, and it does not really make sense to see the ultimate significance of sacrifice in the role of the mediator between the two principals involved.

The differences between the sacrifices are located in the third part of the structure, the meal, and that is an indication that some special significance should be placed on it. In the holocaust only God participates; in the sin offering, God and the priest; in the communion sacrifice, all three, the offerer, the priest, and God. Which of the three sacrifices has priority? In which of them is the full reality of the sacrifice to be found? For the one-act theory of sacrifice, the choice is between the holocaust or the sin offering. In the holocaust, the totality of the offering is symbolized and the honor shown to God is greatest, and either of those aspects could be the central focus of the sacrifice. But we have seen that the ritual of the holocaust reveals it as showing honor to God as the guest at a meal, and it is the meal context that gives meaning to the holocaust. It follows that the holocaust cannot be more important than the meal of which it forms a part. The one-act theory more commonly associates sacrifice with purification from sin, and would see the sin offering as the prototypical sacrifice. This view springs naturally enough from taking the Cross as the primary analogate of sacrifice. The Cross was a sin offering, of that there is no doubt, but that fact alone does not suffice to establish the sin offering as the prototype of sacrifice. The Sacrifice of the Cross is the fulfillment of all the sacrifices of the Old Testament. It is also the New Passover, and the Passover is the fullest of the communion sacrifices. Is there any way of deciding from the ritual of sacrifice which one has priority? Some considerations can be offered.

First, although the sin offering for the whole nation celebrated annually on the Day of Atonement was a very important feast for the Jews, the most important feast each year was the Passover, the national communion sacrifice in which every Israelite must participate, and of all the sacrifices, it is most obvious that the Passover is fundamentally a meal. Our Lord said: "I have eagerly desired to *eat* this Passover with you before I suffer" (Luke 22:15). Further, it is significant that the three sacrifices are very frequently found in combination and almost invariably in the same order, the sin offering, followed by the holocaust, and ending with the communion sacrifice (see, for example, Exodus

29:14, 18, 28; Leviticus 9:15–18). The pattern is not universal, but one can see a logic that might be at work here. The communion sacrifice was forbidden to anyone who was "unclean" and therefore out of communion with God (Leviticus 7:20). So, before he could celebrate, a sin offering was required. The sin offering was a penitential sacrifice preparatory to the communion sacrifice that expressed the fullness of communion with God, its penitential character being the reason why the offerer was required to abstain from the feast. And, finally, it is clear that the most important sacrifice in the Old Testament, the sacrifice that sealed the Covenant, described in Exodus 24, was a meal. "Moses then went up with Aaron, Nadab, Abihu, and seventy elders of Israel, and they beheld the God of Israel. Under his feet there appeared to be sapphires, as clear as the sky itself. Yet he did not smite the chosen men of Israel. They beheld God, and ate and drank" (Exodus 24:9–11). These considerations point to the meal as the culminating part of the sacrifice, and the place where the center of gravity of the whole process is to be found. The sin offering is preparatory to the other two sacrifices, and the holocaust is a privileged part of the sacred meal, which finds its fullest expression in the communion sacrifice. The meal is so central to a sacrifice that one would be justified in thinking of a sacrifice precisely as a meal, a sacred meal shared with God.

Before leaving our consideration of the meal theory of sacrifice, one final point can be made. It concerns the overall spirit of sacrifice, the set of associations the word evokes in the mind. This is taken from Yerkes[9] and is so good that it can simply be quoted at length. The word "sacrifice" in modern usage, clearly based on the one-act theory of sacrifice with the Cross in the background as the primary analogate, has the following characteristics:

> What is sacrificed can be material (a fortune, a limb), or immaterial (pleasure, honesty, fidelity, reputation). What is sacrificed must be of value to the one who makes the sacrifice. The sacrifice is effected by the renouncing or giving *up* the valuable thing. The sacrifice is made *by* someone, *of* something, and *for* something, but never *to* anybody. In fact, it is usually destroyed. . . . Because of the basic importance of deprivation and destruction, the idea of sacrifice always denotes sadness and some sort of misfortune. It is always "too bad" that the sacrifice had to be made; it would have been so much better if the boon could have been secured without it. Therefore, we desire to make our sacrifices as small as possible; only a fool

sacrifices more than is necessary, and the sacrifice is senseless if the boon can be obtained otherwise. We compare the cost of the sacrifice with the value of the result obtained. . . . What is gained is presumed to be more valuable than what was sacrificed; . . . In what is called "the supreme sacrifice," the sacrificer gives up everything and obtains nothing.

Yerkes then goes on to outline the contrasting ancient understanding of sacrifice.

The connotation of the modern secular concept of sacrifice is the very opposite to that of the term in all those ancient religions which formed the milieu of early Christianity and furnished the vocabulary with which the early Christians expressed their ideas and their ideals. Despite the many differences of detail, certain common features characterise sacrifice in Hebrew-Jewish, the Greek and the Roman civilisations. [It is] purely religious in meaning, [having] no secular use whatever. The word never connoted reluctance or deprivation or renunciation or sadness or inevitability grimly accepted. Sacrifices were occasions of greatest joy and festivity and thanksgiving, and were gladly performed as expressions of the attitude of men to their gods. Sacrifices were always as large as possible; the larger they could be made, the greater would be the accompanying joy and festivity. They were offered *by* men *to* their gods; a sacrifice not offered to some person was inconceivable. The stress was upon the *giving* and not upon giving *up*. While they were offered to procure boons from the gods, they were frequently offered after the boon had been received, and as expressions of thanksgiving.

Yerkes speaks of the modern secular concept of sacrifice, but it is basically the same concept that is at work in Christian theology. The ancient joyful concept of sacrifice is clearly associated with the idea of a sacrifice as a sacred meal shared with God. That this ancient concept of sacrifice is that of the Bible is brought out by a passage in Deuteronomy where the Lord is instructing the people in the proper approach to sacrifice.

That is not how you are to worship the Lord, your God. Instead, you shall resort to the place which the Lord, your God, chooses out of all your tribes and designates as his dwelling and there you shall bring your holocausts and sacrifices, your tithes and personal contributions, your votive and free-will offerings, and the firstlings of your herds and flocks. There, too, before the Lord, your God, you and your families shall *eat and make merry* over all your undertakings, because the Lord, your God, has blessed you. (Deuteronomy 12:5–7)

Such, then, is the background to the meal theory of sacrifice. Some of the basic evidence in favor of it has been brought forward, but the debate over the validity of the theory cannot be continued here. As a scholarly issue the debate will no doubt continue indefinitely and a final resolution is probably not possible at that level. In theology, however, what will be important is whether the overall concept makes sense of the data of revelation and Christian experience. When we apply this notion of sacrifice to the Last Supper, the Cross, and the Eucharist, its ability to explain the affirmations of faith and to resolve problems that have hitherto resisted previous attempts will be determinative. In the meantime a choice has to be made, and the validity or otherwise of the choice will only become clear in the end. No other understanding of sacrifice has yet satisfied the *sensus fidei*, and we will only finally know what sacrifice is when the mind of the Church finds the one that fits.

---

1. See Maurice de la Taille, sj, *The Mystery of Faith, Book I: The Sacrifice of Our Lord* (London: Sheed & Ward, 1941), 9f., 19ff.

2. One notable exception is Louis Bouyer, "Sacrifice, Meal and Memorial," in Patrick McGoldrick, ed., *Understanding the Eucharist* (Dublin: Gill and Macmillan, 1969), pp. 47–64.

3. A recent defense of the theory is to be found in Alfred Marx, *"Familiarité et transcendance: La fonction du sacrifice d'après l'Ancien Testament,"* in Adrian Schenker, ed., *Studien zu Opfer und Kult im Alten Testament,* (Tübingen, [Mohr,] 1992), 1–13.

4. Influential here are Walter Eichrodt, *Theology of the Old Testament, Volume One,* (London: SCM Press Ltd, 1961), 141ff., and Roland de Vaux, op, *Ancient Israel: Its Life and Institutions* (London: Darton, Longman & Todd, 1961), 449ff.

5. Gayford, *Sacrifice and the Priesthood,* 79–80.

6. Ibid., 10.

7. Marx, *Familiarité et transcendence,* 6.

8. Ibid., 11.

9. Yerkes, *Sacrifice in Greek and Roman Religions and Early Judaism,* 2ff.

Chapter 6

The Sacrifice of the Cross

We are ready now to embark on the application of the model of sacrifice developed thus far to the Sacrifice of the Cross. This is, clearly, a crucial test for the model. We have seen how it fits in an obvious way with the three-part structure of the Eucharist, but it is not at all obvious how it can fit with the Cross, and if it is to be acceptable in Catholic theology, it must do so coherently. What is obvious is that by far the most common approach to understanding the Sacrifice of the Cross has been to interpret it in terms of the one-act model of sacrifice with which we are all familiar. Indeed, we have suggested that the one-act model is, itself, based on what seems to be the obvious understanding of the Sacrifice of the Cross. In the Christian tradition, the efforts to apply the three-part model of the communion sacrifice to the Cross have been few and far between. So far as I know the first attempt was that of Charles de Condren (1588–1641).[1] His major work, *L'Idée du sacerdoce et du sacrifice de Jésus Christ par P. Condren*,[2] contains some of the key points to be presented here, but the interpretation failed to make any lasting impression on Catholic theology. The only other ones I have found are those by Gayford and Hicks[3] from whom I first discovered the possibility of approaching the matter in this way.

Let us recall, to begin with, the overall pattern of the animal sacrifice to which the Sacrifice of the Cross should conform. There are three living actors involved in the sacrifice, the offerer, the victim, and the priest. The killing of the victim is part of the offertory rite of the sacrifice, and is performed by the offerer. The role of the priest begins after the death of the victim, when the blood is released for ceremonial use and the flesh is available to be shared in the meal. The third and final act of the sacrifice, the goal of all that has gone before and constituting the sacrifice in its fullness, is the festive meal shared with God.

Our task now is to undertake to show how we can apply this model to the Sacrifice of the Cross.

The first point to be established is the place of the Cross in the process, and here the difference between the one-act and the three-part models is quite radical. In the one-act model, the death on the Cross is the one act and it is clearly the act of the priest: "It is for the priest to kill the victim."[4] In the three-part model, however, as Gayford explains, the killing of the victim is, in fact, the task of the offerer, not the priest.

In the Priestly Code this is definitely enjoined in the peace offering (Leviticus 3:2) and the sin offering (4:29, 33, etc.), and is probably taken for granted in the burnt offering (1:5), even if the verb here be impersonal, "one shall kill." That this was the normal rule is implied by 2 Chronicles 30:16, 17, where an exception seems to call for explanation. In the public offerings for the whole nation, the victim might be slain by the Levites (see, for example, Ezekiel 44:11) or the priests (as, for example, on the Day of Atonement, Leviticus 16:15), but clearly as representing the sacrificers, and not *qua* priests or Levites. It may be taken for certain that the acknowledged rule at all periods was for the sacrificer to slay the victim.[5]

Ezekiel 44:10–14 is especially instructive on this point. The Lord is punishing the Levites "who departed from me" and who "shall bear the consequences of their sin" (44:10). Their punishment is that "[t]hey shall not longer draw near to me to serve as my priests, nor shall they touch any of my sacred things, or the most sacred things" (44:13), but one of the duties assigned to them is to "slaughter the holocausts and the sacrifices for the people" (44:11). It is implied that the killing of the victim is not a priestly act, but belongs to the offertory of the sacrifice, and it follows, therefore, that the role of the priest only begins after the animal is dead, when he performs his acts of priestly mediation, the ceremonial use of the blood and the serving of the food for the meal.

The Priestly Mediation

We must first examine the implications of this liturgical rubric that the work of the priest does not begin until the victim is dead.[6] Applied to the Cross, this means that Christ did not begin the work of priestly mediation until after his death, and so, in heaven. As Gayford points out:

> It would be quite in accord with the Jewish view of Sacrifice that Our Lord should enter on the Priestly part of His Sacrificial Work after His Death. . . . The exercise of the Priestly office is to be seen in those acts which correspond to the presenting of the Victim's blood and its body, and these acts presuppose the Death as an accomplished fact; indeed, without the Death that has gone before, they would be valueless and even impossible. That Heaven should be the scene, and the Risen and Ascended Life the time, of the Priestly work is the only condition that satisfies the truth of the Sacrifice.[7]

The issue of the heavenly priesthood of Christ has not entered much into the preaching of the Church, and is therefore not well known. The idea of Christ exercising his priesthood, performing the ceremonial "sprinkling" of the blood in heaven, comes as a surprise to most of us who are so accustomed to thinking of the Sacrifice of the Cross as the death of Christ, his offering of himself "to the end." The point has, however, formed part of a long-standing debate on the interpretation of the Letter to the Hebrews. After discussing Christ's new priesthood, according to the order of Melchizedek, in Chapter 7, the letter continues: "The main point of what has been said is this: We have such a high priest, who has taken His seat at the right hand of the throne of the Majesty in heaven, a minister of the sanctuary and of the true tabernacle that the Lord, not man, set up" (8:1–2) It speaks of the sanctuary as the "heavenly sanctuary" (8:5), and then later tells us that "He entered once for all into the sanctuary . . . with His own blood" (9:12). And later again: "For Christ did not enter into a sanctuary made by hands . . . but heaven itself, that He might now appear before God on our behalf" (9:24).

The logic of the three-part model of sacrifice fits well with one of standard interpretations of what the Letter to the Hebrews teaches on this matter, and it provides a solution to a number of perennial problems.

Our Lord immolates himself outside the tabernacle, on earth; there he pays the ransom for sin. But "the sacrifice (its earthly phase, that is) is mentioned only indirectly as the means of gaining entry to the sanctuary" (J. Bonsirven, *Épître aux Hébreux*, p. 384); for it is not completed simply by the outpouring of blood. In the old rite they immolated the victim in order to take its blood through the first sanctuary into God's dwelling; similarly, Christ offers himself in order to go by way of his immolation into the Holy of Holies of the Godhead.[8]

A difficulty in the interpretation of the Letter to the Hebrews is the relationship between Christ's offering of himself on the Cross and his priestly ministry in heaven. Commenting on Hebrews 8:1–5, Durrwell writes:

> The statement could hardly be clearer: the entry into glory is a consecration, and the activity of the risen Christ is a priestly ministry. It does not, however, justify us in considering the Resurrection as Christ's vocation to the priesthood, His first anointing and the commencement of His sacrificial action. This Socinian thesis goes beyond the facts the epistle gives us and even contradicts some of them. So does the similar, mitigated Socinianism which would divide Christ's sacrifice into two phases, the first, opening phase taking place on earth, and the second, more important one, consisting in Christ's offering of Himself in heaven; the epistle does not support this either. We might perhaps maintain the integrity of the sacrifice of the Cross while postulating a heavenly sacrifice, distinct from the bloody sacrifice, which would consist in the offering made by Christ of His work on earth and of His death, but though this would be quite orthodox, the exegesis would suffer (A. Michel, "Jésus Christ," DTC, col. 1339). The epistle in fact recognises only one sacrifice, the sacrifice of the Cross. . . . Christ was, then, a priest. . . . We come up against statements that appear contrary: the entry into glory is the consecration of the priest, and yet the priesthood is included in the sonship he already possessed.[9]

According to Durrwell, Hebrews does not support the idea that the Sacrifice of the Cross could take place in phases. He offers no texts to corroborate the assertion, so it is not possible to verify or deny it at the level of exegesis. However, that is precisely the interpretation which the model of sacrifice we are working with demands. There is, indeed, "only one sacrifice, the sacrifice of the Cross," but that sacrifice takes place in three parts, of which the priestly mediation is the second, taking place after the death. Again, according to Durrwell, "the entry into glory is a consecration," and again no text is offered in support. The model of sacrifice we are dealing with would say that Christ begins to exercise his priestly ministry on his entry into glory, not that he begins to be a priest. In the national sin offering on Yom Kippur,

the high priest performs the offering of the animal, but he only begins
to act as priest when he enters the Holy of Holies for the sprinkling
of the blood. Parallel with this, in the case of Christ's sacrifice, there is
no problem about his being a priest on the Cross. What is important
is that he only begins the priestly part of the sacrifice in heaven. Nothing,
therefore, need "appear contrary." The parallel is exact. Christ was
always a priest according to the order of Melchizedek, but he began
his work of priestly mediation after he rose from the dead.

A second difficulty is the eternity of Christ's priesthood.
Durrwell writes: "Among the new aspects of Christ's priesthood, the
light of eternity on His face particularly interests the author. Christ's
glorification places His priestly activity in the 'eternal now' of God;
this is affirmed over and over again (5:6; 6:20; 7:3, 8, 16–17, 20–28) and
is the essential point of comparison between Christ and [Melchizedek,
7:3]. . . ."[10] There can be no doubt on this basic point; the difficulty
lies in explaining how it can be. Durrwell explains the problem
at some length.

> The mediating activity of the priest reaches its high point in that exchange
> of gifts between God and men which constitutes a sacrifice. Hence the
> question: Does the priesthood of glory include a sacrifice as the priesthood
> of blood did before? The epistle certainly seems to deny this categorically,
> recognising only one oblation, consummated once and for all. Yet the
> problem of a sacrifice in heaven has worried all the commentators; whatever
> their answer, the very fact that they are so preoccupied with it proves that
> it is a problem that must be faced. There is a *liturgy* in heaven whose
> celebrant is Christ: 8:1–5.[11] . . . If we are to make this text fit in with the
> absolute uniqueness of Christ's sacrifice in both number and kind, which
> we believe, we must allow that the mystery of the Cross is prolonged in
> eternity. In the thought of this epistle, the Christian sacrifice was not a deed
> which took place and was wholly completed in time, so that only the merit
> remains. In the author's mind, the act of offering is eternal and heavenly,
> because it becomes eternal in itself, and is prolonged in Christ's existence
> in glory.[12] . . . It is the blood itself, Christ actually being pierced, that
> cleanses our souls. . . . Yet we have to reconcile the need for a unique
> sacrifice with the need for continuity; this can only be met by the eternal
> permanence of the victim in the ever-actual acceptance of God. . . .
> Though the sacrificial act took place in the past, its conclusion is something
> ever actual in the everlasting glorifying welcome of God. The act of
> passing from this world to the Father took place once for all, but the

meeting with the Father continues forever: the victim is fixed eternally at the high point of the offering.[13]

For Durrwell, the eternity of Christ's sacrifice of which the Letter to the Hebrews speaks must imply the eternity of his death. "In the ever-actual permanence of His glorification, Christ's death itself thus remains eternal in its actuality, fixed at its final point, at the moment of its perfection."[14] Others also have tried to resolve the problem along these lines. Odo Casel's famous *Mysteriengegenwart* theory is just the most famous of the efforts made to make sense of the eternity of Christ's sacrifice in the mysterious eternity of his death. Durrwell, however, does admit that "many minds seem to find an insoluble enigma in this permanence of an ever-actual immolation in the midst of a life of glory. . . ."[15] And so they do. Edward Schillebeeckx makes the determinative point against this approach. "First, time itself is irreversible. Whatever is historically past cannot now, in any way at all, be made once more actually present, not even by God himself, not even 'in mystery.' Whatever has happened in the history is irrevocably past and done. A fact historically past cannot therefore be actualised anew mystically or in the sacrament."[16] Schillebeeckx here points out, quite rightly, that every historical event belongs to one place and one time, and simply cannot be rendered eternally enduring by any act of understanding. What is past is past. However, he still seeks to find an eternity in Christ's death. "But if in the sacraments there is nevertheless a certain presence in mystery, this is possible only if, in Christ's historical redemptive acts, there already was an element of something perennial; an enduring trans-historical element which now becomes sacramentalized in an earthly event in our own time in a visible act of the Church."[17] And he goes on: "Since the sacrifice of the Cross and all the mysteries of the life of Christ are personal acts of God, they are eternally actual and enduring. God the Son himself is present in these human acts in a manner that transcends time. For of course we cannot conceive of the presence of a mere act; presence in this kind of context is always the presence of the person who acts; a personal presence which renders itself actual here and now, and active in and through an act."[18] What Schillebeeckx says here is undoubtedly true. Since Christ as God is eternal, his divine act is eternal, but it does not establish the eternity of the human act of Christ on the Cross, his sacrifice, which is what the Letter to the Hebrews teaches. Durrwell is correct when he says: "In the thought of this epistle, the Christian sacrifice was not a deed which took place and was wholly completed in time, so that only the merit remains,"[19] and this is effectively what Schillebeeckx is affirming, so that Schillebeeckx, while stating an important truth, is not solving the problem. What the Hebrews teaches is precisely the eternity of the sacrifice.

All these difficulties find their origin in one and the same source, the presuppositions of the one-act model of sacrifice. If once the three-part model is brought to bear on the question, the difficulties resolve themselves quite simply. One important point to be brought out in order to unravel the tangle which the one-act model involves is the true interpretation of the role of the blood in an animal sacrifice. Durrwell speaks for the whole tradition which he represents when he writes: "It is the blood itself, Christ actually being pierced, that cleanses our souls." Hence, if sacrifice that cleanses our souls is to be eternal, the very piercing must be eternal, and so "Christ's death itself thus remains eternal in its actuality." On the one-act model of sacrifice, the blood is the death.

Now in the three-part model of sacrifice the death and the blood are understood quite differently from this. For the one-act model of sacrifice, the death is the one act. With the Cross as primary analogate, how could it be otherwise? We are redeemed by Christ's death, and any satisfactory understanding of the Sacrifice of the Cross must account for the role of his death as the act which brought about our salvation. It is a different question, however, to ask what is the function of the death within the structure of a sacrifice. The Sacrifice of the Cross is a unique case, and it is not correct to judge all sacrifice on the basis of this one example. The question still remains to be asked on the basis of the evidence of the actual liturgy of the Temple sacrifices, and an examination of the texts does not support the notion that the death of the victim occupies the central place in the sacrificial rite that the one-act model of sacrifice implies. Gayford points out that "if the killing of the victim occupied such a central position in the ceremonial of Sacrifice, we should expect to find the ceremonial rubrics of the Law laying a particular stress upon this act. But, on the contrary, there is less detail prescribed in regard to this than to any of the other acts."[20] Outside the priestly texts, there are dozens of texts that

speak of the offering of a sacrifice, but only Genesis 22:10 and
1 Samuel 1:25 mention it, which would hardly be the case if it were
the central act of the whole process. Yerkes, in speaking of the Greek
thusia makes a similar point, and there is no reason to suppose that
the basic understanding of sacrifice was not the same as in the sacrifices
of Israel. "The slaying, flaying and dissecting of the victims required
the longest time for performance and the fewest words for description.
The operations were necessary for every flesh meal and, of course,
for every thusia, but they were never given any sort of religious significance or interpretation."[21]

In fact, in the three-part model of sacrifice the meaning of
the death can be determined exactly. It is simply the necessary means
required to make the flesh of the animal available as food, just as for
any other meal where meat is eaten. Evidence for this interpretation is
the very word used for the animal communion sacrifice, *zevach*. As
Yerkes tells us: "The root of the word *zevach* is found in practically every
semitic language; it expressed not the simple idea of killing or slaying,
but the idea of preparing an animal for eating."[22] This has obvious
implications for the interpretation of the role of the death of the
animal. "Slaying for sacrifice was naturally performed with solemnity
proper for the occasion, but no significance was ever attached to the
fact that the animal had died. We never hear of death *qua* death
effecting anything."[23] On the three-part model of sacrifice, it is clear
that the death of the animal cannot be considered the "one act" constituting the sacrifice. The death is, rather, the means to an end, and the
end and culmination of the sacrifice is the meal. This vision is contained in the very word "victim." In modern English, the word "victim"
has the primary technical meaning of an animal offered in sacrifice,
and the secondary, metaphorical usage, derived from the common
understanding of a sacrifice, of a person unjustly treated in some way.
The word has lost any link with its original connection to the verb
vivo, vivere, victus, "to live," where the past participle, *victus*, is used as
a noun to mean, precisely, "food." This original meaning is continued
in the English verb, "to victual," meaning "to supply with food." So, in
its traditional meaning, a victim is not an innocent suffering injustice,
but an animal that is prepared as food, a source of life.

This basic significance of the death of the animal as being the
means of making its flesh available as food was common to all ancient

sacrifices, just as to all flesh meals. However, the death of the animal has a second effect that is of great importance in the sacrifices of Israel, the release of the blood. There is a great mystique about blood in the Bible. For us the blood is an essential principle of life, but for the Hebrews it was more, it was *the actual life itself*: "The blood is the life" (Deuteronomy 12:23). Gayford tells us that:

> [i]t is not too much to say that the Hebrews regarded the life-blood almost as a living thing inside the body which it quickened; and not only was it the vitalising life while it pulsated within the body, but it had an independent life of its own, even when taken from the body. . . . To us moderns blood, and particularly blood that has been shed, brings up the associations of death; to the Hebrews it meant life that has passed indeed through the experience of death, but has not itself been killed by that experience: it still lives.[24]

Again in this case, we find that it is not death *qua* death, in the sense of the loss of life, which is significant, but death as the means of releasing the blood which could then be used within the priestly mediation. This is a second reason pointing to the fact that the death cannot possibly be seen as the "one act" constitutive of sacrifice, but a means leading to the priestly acts of the liturgy, the ceremonial use of the blood and the serving of the sacred meal.

However, once the idea is proposed it seems obvious enough. The ceremonial use of the blood is only possible after the victim is dead and the blood is released. And the value of the blood explains the meaning of the death. As Hicks puts it: "To us, with our modern associations, [blood] is merely the evidence, the revolting evidence, of slaughter and destruction. To the men of the ancient world it was not revolting, but precious. It was life, once prisoned and misused, now released. It was more than that. It was the life which was at once their own and God's, the holiest thing, therefore, that they knew."[25] In the New Testament writings, in almost every case, it is the blood of Christ which saves us and not so much his death, for his death was seen as the source of the life, which is in the blood. And Hicks again: "It is not the death that atones, but the life. The death is vital to the sacrifice, because it sets free the blood, which is the life. But the victim is, in a true sense, operative, not as dead, but as alive 'as it had been slain' . . . [for] the death is only made effective when the work of the blood begins,

THE SACRIFICE OF THE CROSS

and after, or with, it the further stages also."[26] So, the death of Christ, like any death in the context of a sacrifice, is not seen in the tragic terms we take for granted. It was not a tragic loss of life, but the glorious release of the life within, and the true life begins afterwards. His death is not seen as the separation of soul and body which we consider so tragic, but the separation of the body and blood, the freeing of the life to be shared and the flesh to be eaten, the blood to be drunk. What is so tragic about the separation of the soul and the body, since it simply meant the end of his suffering and the beginning of eternal glory?

On this perspective opened up by the three-part model of sacrifice, the problem of the eternity of the sacrifice disappears. The sacrifice is quite obviously eternal. The death of Christ on the Cross is the first of three acts in the sacrifice. It is the offertory of the sacrifice that is preparatory to the properly priestly acts that begin afterward, and these acts, the priestly mediation of Christ's intercession at the right hand of the Father and the serving of the sacred meal to follow are, of their very nature, eternal. There is no need of any mysterious theory to explain how Christ's session at His Father's right hand and the banquet of eternal life are eternal. They simply are, and they are the parts of the Sacrifice of the Cross that last forever. There is, therefore, no need at all for the death of Christ to be eternal, other than the eternity of any historical event, which once it happens, always has happened. Christ's death was "once for all" and its effects are eternal, but the eternity of the Sacrifice of the Cross is the plain eternity of the resurrected life of Christ in heaven. There is no doubt that there is "only one oblation, consummated once and for all." However, on the three-part model of sacrifice, this does not deny a priesthood of glory in the least. As we have already seen, it demands a priesthood of glory, for it is only in glory that the priesthood can begin.

THE OFFERTORY OF THE SACRIFICE

Once this heavenly perspective is opened up, the whole aspect of the Sacrifice of the Cross is transformed. It can no longer be seen as a one-act offering beginning and ending on the Cross, but must be interpreted in the light of the three-part structure of the Temple sacrifices, and these further implications need to be examined. If the priestly mediation takes place in heaven, it follows that the Passion of Christ must belong to the offertory of the Sacrifice of the Cross, for the killing of the victim is the work of the offerer and not the priest. Recall that, in principle, the offerer and the priest are two distinct actors in a sacrifice. What the priest does is also called "offering" sacrifice, but in the sense that the word is normally understood as implying a gift of one's property symbolizing the gift of oneself, this "offering" belongs to the offerer, not the priest. The priest is a mediator "offering" the sacrifice on behalf of another, the offerer. When we come to examine the offertory, it is the primary offering, the gift of self that we are interested in.

A first point to notice is that in the offertory there are two actors, the offerer and the victim, and in the Passion it is Christ's role as victim that is the more in evidence. On the Cross he is the Lamb of God, and for the Bible a lamb meant inevitably a lamb of sacrifice. As Gayford remarks: "The office of Victim is so frequently expressed or implied of Jesus Christ in the New Testament as hardly to need particular mention."[27] He expressed his acceptance of the role of victim in many ways. The first act of the public life was his baptism, when he publicly committed himself to death in obedience to the Father's will. He often spoke of the death that awaited him, and in the Garden he expressed his acceptance clearly. "My Father, if it is possible let this chalice pass from me; yet, not my will but yours be done" (Matthew 26:39). These are expressions of his acceptance of victimhood.

Now, if Christ is the victim, who is the offerer? On the one-act model, it was always taken for granted that Christ was everything, offerer, victim, and priest, and that is true enough. We have already pointed out that the dominant idea in Western theology has been that of Christ offering himself as a holocaust to the Father. "Christ loved us and handed Himself over as an offering and sacrifice to God in the odour of sweetness" (Ephesians 5:2). The question then is: When and how did he offer the Sacrifice of the Cross? Did he positively offer the Sacrifice of the Cross on any occasion? This was de la Taille's question, and his answer was that Christ offered the Sacrifice of the Cross at the Last Supper. There has to be some truth in that, but the problem with it is that it confuses the two orders, the sacramental and the real. At the Last Supper, our Lord was offering a communion sacrifice of bread and wine as a sacrament of his Universal Sacrifice, and implicitly expressing his sacrificial will in view of the Cross. But is it appropriate to consider this the formal moment of offering himself to his death on the Cross?

A better answer to the question possibly comes to light if we expand the horizon somewhat, guided once again by the three-part model of sacrifice. The three-part model calls for another offerer distinct from the victim. Essential to the act of offering is that one offer something of one's own as a gift. Is there anyone else who could be legitimately thought of as possessing proprietary rights over the Lamb of God, such that it would make sense to speak of offering him? The obvious candidate here is God the Father. Could it be that He is offering His Son in sacrifice? There is a very good reason to suggest that it is so. At his baptism, God the Father says to Jesus: "You are my beloved Son." This phrase has two Old Testament references. It refers to the Servant Songs of Isaiah, "my servant . . . in whom my soul delights" (Isaiah 42:1), and, which is of particular interest here, Abraham's sacrifice of Isaac. God told Abraham to take his "beloved" son (Genesis 22:2) and offer him as a holocaust on Mount Moriah. Abraham was willing to obey the Lord's command and prepared to offer his son, but God stopped him short of completing the sacrifice. However, Abraham had prophesied that "God Himself will provide the sheep for the holocaust" (Genesis 22:8), and now that prophecy is fulfilled. Now God the Father is doing precisely what He asked of Abraham in offering His own Son in sacrifice to us. Surely this is the perspective which explains why Saint John in his Gospel has no baptism of Jesus, and instead of baptizing Jesus, John the Baptist says "Behold the Lamb of God, who takes away the sin of the world" (John 1:29). Saint John is interpreting the baptism as the moment of the offertory of the Sacrifice of the Cross, when the Father offers His Son to us and Jesus willingly accepts his role as victim of the sacrifice, just as Isaac did. The primary offerer of the Sacrifice of the Cross, therefore, is God the Father, and this can only make sense on the meal theory of sacrifice. The Father cannot offer a holocaust in honor of Himself, or make an offering for sins, but He can offer His Son to us as the Bread of Life, to be shared in the sacred meal that lasts forever.

The three-part model invites us to push further still. Recalling that it is the task of the offerer to kill the victim of a sacrifice, we need to ask the question, Who killed him?, for whoever killed him must somehow have been involved in the offertory of the Sacrifice of the

Cross. The Gospels, and Saint Matthew in particular, emphasize the fact that he was killed by the Jews, led by the high priest, Caiaphas. Indeed, Saint Matthew insists on the point so strongly that he has been accused of anti-Semitism. Now, these new perspectives lead us to suggest that Matthew had something much more profound in mind, which is quite the reverse of anti-Semitism. The Sacrifice of the Cross is also the fulfillment of the two national sacrifices of Israel, the Passover and the sin offering on the Day of Atonement. What is special about them is that they are offered by the whole people. The Passover is offered family by family, and the national sin offering is offered by the high priest on behalf of the nation as a whole. Here is an alternative possibility as to the source of Saint Matthew's insistence. He is making the point that the high priest and the whole people of Israel are, all unwittingly, offering the national sacrifices in a way that fulfills them both. This is the fulfillment of all the promises, for Israel is offering the Lamb of God to take away the sins of the world. They are making the sin offering of the last Day of Atonement and offering the New Passover. The people's prophecy, "His blood be upon us and upon our children" (Matthew 27:25), is not a claim of blood guilt but a prayer for salvation. This is a Matthean irony as deep and profound as that of Saint John when he had Caiaphas prophesy "that it is better for you that one man should die for the people, and that the whole nation should not perish" (John 11:50).

And, of course, the Jews were not alone. Jesus was directly killed by the Gentiles, the Romans, so they were somehow involved in the offertory of Christ's sacrifice. In fact, the New Testament accounts of what happened make clear that there was a general conspiracy leading to the Cross. In the Passion narratives the initiator of the process that led to the death of Jesus is Judas, the betrayer, which means literally, "the one who handed him over." Judas handed him over to the chief priests (Matthew 26:15), who handed him over to Pilate (27:2), who in turn handed him over to the soldiers for crucifixion (27:26). The importance of Judas in the story, the reason he figures so prominently in the Passion accounts, is not that he "betrayed" Jesus, but that he "handed him over." He was one of the very apostles, one of Christ's own followers, and it was he who began the final act of the offertory of the Paschal Sacrifice. And the overall point being made, surely, is that everyone, Christian, Jew, and Gentile, was implicated in the death of Jesus, and that, therefore, all were involved, all unwittingly, in the offertory of the Paschal Sacrifice.

Did anyone offer the sacrifice willingly with Christ? At the Last Supper Jesus was offering himself as the Lamb of the New Passover and inviting the apostles to offer themselves with him, by drinking his cup. Peter promised that he would stay with Jesus unto death, but of course he didn't. Only one of the apostles stayed faithful to the end; John the beloved disciple who was there at the foot of the Cross, together with Our Lady and the other women. They were the only ones co-offering with Jesus at the time, forerunners of all of us in the Church who are called to join ourselves to the Sacrifice in our turn. However, the fact remains that all were involved whether they liked it or not.

So, in answer to the question, Who offered the Sacrifice of the Cross? it turns out that everyone did and still does. In this way the point is made that everyone without exception is a co-offerer of this Sacrifice, Christians, Jews, and Gentiles. We all cooperate whether we know it or not, whether we like it or not, one way or the other. The profound phrase from an old Act of Contrition is applicable here. We express our sorrow that our sins "have crucified our loving Savior Jesus Christ." And that is the truth of the matter. We are all involved in the offertory of the Sacrifice of the Cross. By our sins we all killed him. And how could it be otherwise? We are the sinners, we are the ones who needed to offer the sin offering, not him. So, in so far as we are sinners, we have a hand in his death; in so far as we do the will of God, we are co-redeemers with Christ, offering ourselves through him, with him, and in him, for the salvation of the world. This sacrifice is cosmic in its scope, and includes everyone, every human being who has ever lived or will live, it is coextensive with the history of salvation.

THE MEAL

So far we have seen the first two parts of the three-part model of sacrifice verified in Christ's sacrifice, the offertory on the Cross and the priestly mediation taking place afterward in heaven. What, then, is to be said of the third part, the sacred meal shared with God? The logic of the structure is not difficult to discern. Surely everything points to the simple fact that the third part of Christ's sacrifice, the meal, which must take place after the priestly mediation, is the banquet of eternal life in heaven.

In this we see the fulfillment of the most fundamental of all Israelite sacrifices, the covenant sacrifice on Mount Sinai. Christ's sacrifice was a covenant sacrifice, establishing the New Covenant. In Israel the solemn declaration of a covenant was formally confirmed by a meal, as for example in Genesis 26:28–30; 31:44–54. This was what happened when God made the covenant with His people at Mount Sinai as recorded in Exodus 24. Moses "built an altar at the foot of the mountain . . . and he sent young men of the people of Israel, who offered burnt offerings and sacrificed peace offerings of oxen to the Lord" (vv. 4, 5). He then performed the act of priestly mediation, throwing half of the blood against the altar and throwing the rest upon the people (vv. 6–8). Finally, Moses and Aaron and the elders of Israel went up Mount Sinai where "they beheld God, and ate and drank" (v. 11). The three parts of a sacrifice are verified here in this fundamental sacrifice establishing God's covenant with Israel, the offertory, the priestly mediation, and the meal. In Christ's sacrifice, where the offertory is on the Cross, and the priestly mediation is Christ's eternal intercession in heaven, the meal that seals the New and eternal Covenant can only be the banquet of eternal life.

Durrwell has made this point well.

"I say to you, I will not drink from henceforth of the fruit of the vine, until that day when I shall drink it with you, new, in the kingdom of My Father." (Mt. 26:29; Mk. 14:25) These words herald the great messianic banquet . . . The Eucharist appears as the earthly anticipation of the feast to be celebrated in the joy of the new wine in the Kingdom. . . . It will be on "that day", at the end of time, that the feast will be eaten, and in the Kingdom of the Father. Now, for Christ the final day is the day of His glorification, and the Kingdom begins with His entry into glory. That is the moment when Christ sits down at the table of His sacrifice. The disciples will then take their places in turn. They will gather round their risen Master in a mysterious feast. They will communicate in the Redemption, united to Christ in glory, and receiving, in Him, the glorifying action of God.[28] . . . All this combines to identify the inauguration of the messianic banquet with the resurrection of the Lord, and to define His glory as a paschal meal, a communion in the Cross. . . . In the light of sacrificial theory, the glorification of Christ appears as a necessary phase of His oblation. It is the completion without which His sacrifice is essentially mutilated and is therefore no sacrifice—just as there can be no movement which does not arrive anywhere, and no gift where there is no one to accept it. His glorification not only completes His sacrifice in itself, but also makes it beneficial: in the divinized victim God communicates Himself to the offerer and to all who eat at the altar.[29]

The meal theory of sacrifice demands this wide perspective. The sacred meal is not only an essential part of a sacrifice, but its culminating point. On this approach the whole atmosphere of the Cross is changed. The Cross loses its tragic, sad, and ominous aspect, and becomes more clearly related to the Resurrection. There has been a strong effort in Catholic theology in recent decades to recover the importance of the Resurrection in the work of our salvation. It seemed to be that a choice had to be made between the Cross and the Resurrection, between the emphasis on sacrifice and the emphasis on joy. But if the three-part model of sacrifice is accepted, the dichotomy disappears. A sacrifice is a joyful meal shared with God, and the Cross is seen for what it is, a necessary preparation for the joyful meal to follow. Christ offering sacrifice does not refer primarily to his sacrificial death, necessary and fundamental as it is, but also and essentially to the two acts of the sacrifice that follow the death, his intercession at the Father's right hand and the banquet of eternal life. The banquet of eternal life is the Universal Sacrifice of Christ, the Sacrifice of the Cross.

We set out to see if the three-part model of sacrifice could be coherently applied to the Sacrifice of the Cross, and we believe that it can. This alternative model opens up perspectives that, while being substantially obscured by the one-act model, turn out to have a solid base in scripture and Tradition, so that the three-part model of sacrifice can be considered to have passed this essential test of its applicability to Christian sacrifice.

---

1. Lepin, *L'Idée du sacrifice de la Messe d'après les théologiens* (Paris: Gabriel Beauchesne, 1926), 471–472.

2. Quoted in Lepin, *L'Idée du sacrifice de la Messe d'après les théologiens.*

3. Gayford, *Sacrifice and the Priesthood*, 123ff.; Hicks, *The Fullness of Sacrifice*, 236ff.

4. Saint Thomas, ST III, 22, 2, obj. 1: *Sacerdotis enim est hostiam occidere.*

5. Gayford, *Sacrifice and the Priesthood,* 64–65.

6. Ibid. 144ff., Hicks, *The Fullness of Sacrifice,* 240.

7. Gayford, *Sacrifice and the Priesthood,* 149–150.

8. F. X. Durrwell, CSSR, *The Resurrection* (London/Melbourne/New York: Sheed and Ward, 1960), 66.

9. Ibid., 138.

10. Ibid, 139.

11. Ibid., 142–143.

12. Ibid., 143–144.

13. Ibid., 145.

14. Ibid., 149.

15. Ibid., 148.

16. Edward Schillebeeckx, OP, *Christ the Sacrament of Encounter with God* (New York: Sheed and Ward, 1963), 55.

17. Ibid., 56.

18. Ibid., 57.

19. Durrwell, *The Resurrection,* 143.

20. Gayford, *Sacrifice and the Priesthood,* 106.

21. Yerkes, *Sacrifice in Greek and Roman Religions and Early Judaism,* 104.

22. Ibid., 147.

23. Ibid., 5. Yerkes observes that this point was first noted by H. C. Turnbull, *The Blood Covenant* (1893), 286. There is no way Yerkes could have known that the point was made two centuries earlier by Condren.

24. Gayford, *Sacrifice and the Priesthood,* 68–69.

25. Hicks, *The Fullness of Sacrifice,* 242.

26. Hicks, *The Fullness of Sacrifice,* 18, 243.

27. Gayford, *Sacrifice and the Priesthood,* 138.

28. Durrwell, *The Resurrection,* 75.

29. Ibid., 76.

Chapter 7

The Sacramental Sacrifice

We come now to the last stage of our investigation when we apply the results attained to the Liturgy of the Eucharist. We have presented the three-part model of sacrifice discerned in the sacrifices of Israel. We have seen how this model fits easily with the structure of the Eucharist, when the Offertory and Communion are taken as essential elements of the Eucharistic sacrifice together with the Eucharistic Prayer. We have applied the model to the Sacrifice of the Cross and found that certain perspectives were opened up that turned out to be quite traditional although unable to be properly integrated into Western Catholic theology for many centuries. We try now to put the bits together and see how the different aspects help to interpret each other.

ONE SACRIFICE/MANY SACRIFICES

Our first task is to tackle the long-standing issue of the mystery involved in affirming an apparently independent daily sacrifice of the Eucharist with the datum of faith that the Sacrifice of Christ is one, offered once and for all on Calvary. Can we affirm a liturgical sacrifice of the Eucharist and avoid affirming a second sacrifice in competition with the one Sacrifice of the Cross? Different points help us to unravel this issue. We pointed out earlier that the Tridentine discussion gives some pointers toward a solution of the fundamental difficulty that causes all the problems, and the development of the understanding of a sacramental sacrifice is undoubtedly also a help.

At Bologna in August 1547, some of the theologians responded directly to the Lutheran assertion that the Eucharist is not a sacrifice but only a commemoration of the Sacrifice of the Cross. Six spoke directly to the point, but only three managed to make the clear rebuttal that the Eucharist is not only a commemoration of the Sacrifice of the Cross, but a sacrifice that is celebrated in commemoration of the Sacrifice of the Cross. One affirmed: "that the offering in the Mass is a commemoration of the Sacrifice of the Cross, but not only a commemoration, but also a sacrifice, and this sacrifice is a memorial of the Sacrifice of the Cross."[1] At Trent in 1551, three theologians spoke to this point, and this time only one, the famous Melchior Cano, managed to state explicitly that "if we do not offer and sacrifice, we do not represent the Sacrifice of Christ offered on the Cross."[2] Now, all we have to do is substitute "sacrament" for "commemoration" in these statements, and all the problems disappear. It is the sacrifice of the Eucharist that is the sacrament of the Sacrifice of the Cross. And Saint Cyprian said as much long ago in his letter to Caecilium, when he wrote: "Likewise, in the priest Melchisedech, we see the sacrament of the sacrifice of the Lord prefigured."[3] And Saint Augustine, too, was surely thinking along these lines when he wrote to Boniface: "Was Christ not immolated once in Himself, and still in the Sacrament, not only at every paschal solemnity but every day He is immolated by the people, nor does he lie who responds to the question that He is immolated? *If, indeed sacraments do not have some similarity to the things of which they are sacraments, then they are not sacraments at all.*"[4] The Eucharist is the sacrament of the Sacrifice of the Cross, and that is why there are not two sacrifices, but only one. The same idea is implied when it is asserted that in the Eucharist we offer sacrifice "under the appearances of bread and wine." The same mystery of transubstantiation is at work here as in the transformation of the bread and wine into the Body and Blood of Christ. Just as the bread and wine become the Body and Blood of Christ, so the sacrifice of the bread and wine becomes the Sacrifice of the Cross. The Eucharist has all the appearances of a sacrifice. It looks like a sacrifice, it sounds like a sacrifice, it is acted out like a sacrifice, and on the natural level it is a sacrifice. However, by the mystery of transubstantiation it is not longer merely a natural sacrifice, but the one supernatural Sacrifice of the Cross. In every outward quality we celebrate it as a sacrifice, and it is the power of God that transforms it into the Sacrifice of the Cross.

And this answers Vonier's objection. He said that "[i]t is of utmost importance, in order to safeguard the sacramentality of the sacrifice of the Mass, to eliminate from it all such things as would make it into a natural sacrifice, a human act, with human sensations and human circumstances."[5] Now, it is clearly impossible to remove from the Eucharist all that would make it "a human act, with human sensations and human circumstances," for in that case we would have to do nothing at all. So, if there must be a human act of some kind, and we must do something liturgical in order to worship, why should it not be a sacrifice? Why should a sacrifice compete with the Cross any more than any other liturgical celebration one might devise? And Melchior Cano's point is a valid one. The obvious—he called it the necessary—sacrament of the Sacrifice of the Cross is itself a sacrifice. The value of the development of the sacramental sacrifice idea has allowed us finally to separate the two orders, the natural and the sacramental, and so we can finally see that in the Eucharist there are not two sacrifices, but one sacrifice that is actual on the two levels, the natural and the sacramental. The natural sacrifice of bread and wine is full and perfect in its own right, and that full and perfect, natural sacrifice is a sacrament of Christ's Universal Sacrifice, and is thereby transformed into that cosmic sacrifice. The true and proper sacrifice of bread and wine is repeated daily, and on each occasion it becomes the one Sacrifice of Christ. This is the true understanding of the Eucharist as a sacramental sacrifice. It is not that some unspecified religious ritual of prayer is a sacrament realizing the one Sacrifice of Christ. Rather it is a true and proper sacrifice of bread and wine that is the sacramental sign of the one Universal Sacrifice. With this understanding of the matter we return to the simple intuition of faith that was possible before the medieval theologians had complicated matters, for this point was made a long time ago in a short summary of the faith produced at the end of the eleventh century. "Although with my bodily eyes I see a priest at the altar of the Lord offering bread and wine, however, with the eyes of faith and the pure light in my heart, I see the High Priest himself, the true Pontiff, our Lord Jesus Christ offering himself."[6] And surely it makes more sense that the Eucharist would be sacrificial on both levels. What better sign of the perfect sacrifice could there be than a simple communion sacrifice of bread and wine that sums up and fulfils all that is contained in the sacrificial system of Israel? Our Lord came not to abolish all that had gone before but to complete it.

This duality in the Eucharist has been adverted to at different times. For instance, Rupert de Deutz observed: "It is not only, therefore, the bread and wine which are seen bodily which the Church offers, but also the Word and the Son of God."[7] For him the matter of the sacrifice is double, made up of terrestrial and heavenly matter: on the one hand, the bread, on the other the Word, the God-bearing bread.[8] More recently, a commentator on the liturgy of the Eucharist had this to say.

> Research into the Eucharist seems to bring us into two very different "climates." The first of these might be called, very roughly, "natural" . . . In this "climate" the essence of the Eucharist seems to consist in the *dona*, and if we confined ourselves to interpreting the *sacrifice* of the Mass in terms of the liturgy's use of "offer" and cognate expressions, we should be led, surely, to see this sacrifice as the offering to God of gifts—bread and wine, and other foodstuffs destined to supply the church with her material needs. It is not surprising to find non-Catholic scholars seeing in these offerings, which occupy the greater part of the *secreta*, the origin of the whole conception of the Mass as sacrifice (Wetter). The other climate we get into not (or certainly, far less) by contact with the texts, but through the study of the *theology* of the Eucharist as this theology developed later. In this world of thought we soon find ourselves taking it for granted that the Eucharist is a sacrifice through its connection (to be deliberately vague) with Calvary. Between these two climates there seems to be an enormous gulf. It is as though we had to choose, as between two quite different atmospheres, which one we are going to live in and think in.[9]

On the position being proposed here, this perception of Moore turns out to be completely accurate. There are indeed two "climates" in the Eucharist; the sacrifice is realized on two distinct levels. However, we do not have to choose between them. We must affirm both clearly, distinguishing them in order to understand exactly how they relate to each other. So the Eucharist needs to be considered on two levels. It needs to be understood, first of all, as a sacrifice in its own right, with all that that implies, and then, in a second moment, the sacramental reality is to be discerned.

THE NATURAL SACRIFICE

The Distinction of Priesthoods

We first of all examine the Eucharist as a true and proper, full and
perfect, natural sacrifice of bread and wine. It is on this first level
that a number of long-standing difficulties find their resolution. First
of all there is the question of the identity of the Catholic priesthood,
and how the ministerial priesthood differs from the universal
priesthood of the laity. Ever since Luther's denial of the visible
priesthood of the ordained minister, Catholic theology has been hard
pressed to explain clearly how it is that the president of the Eucharist
is, in fact, a true priest in the liturgical sense. Though the Church
has no doubt that the universal and the ministerial priesthoods "differ
essentially and not only in degree" (LG 10), a clear and easily
discerned reason for the distinction has not been forthcoming. While
the whole meaning of the Eucharistic sacrifice is focused on the
Eucharistic Prayer, in which all join in spirit, the distinction is
not so easy to see. However, on the model of sacrifice presented here,
the distinction is obvious. When the Eucharist is understood to be
a natural sacrifice of bread and wine, the priestly character of the
president of the Eucharist is as obvious as the priestly character of any
of the sons of Levi ministering in the Temple in Jerusalem. When the
Eucharist is understood as a sacrifice in exactly the same sense as
any of the sacrifices of Israel, the whole difficulty is resolved. The
president of the Eucharist, when he comes to the Eucharistic Prayer,
is acting as the priestly mediator between God and humanity in
exactly the same way as the priests of the Old Testament. The common
priesthood of all the Christian faithful is then seen to be identical in
character with the common priesthood of all the faithful of Israel
mentioned in Exodus 19:6: "you shall be to me a kingdom of priests. . . ."
The Christian laity exercise their priesthood just as did the whole
people of Israel, by their offering of the sacrifice in their proper order.
So, the priest (*presbyter*) is not simply a sacramental priest (*hiereus*)
by his acting "in the person of Christ," just as the Eucharist is not
simply a sacramental sacrifice. The two problems are parts of the same
problem, so that when the true and proper sacrificial nature of the
Eucharist is discerned, the sacrificial priesthood of the ordained
minister is obvious.

The Double Offering

Another vexed question is the manner of relating the exercise of the common and ministerial priesthood in the actual celebration of the Eucharist. There is a long tradition in the Church that the Eucharist is the offering of the whole Church. The point was strongly emphasised by Saint John Chrysostom.

> But there are occasions in which there is no difference at all between the priest and those under him; for instance, when we are to partake of the awful mysteries; for we are all alike counted worthy of the same things; not as under the Old Testament [when] the priest ate some things and those under him others, and it was not lawful for the people to partake of those things whereof the priest partook. But not so now, but before all one body is set and one cup. . . . The offering of thanksgiving again is common: for neither does he give thanks alone, but also all the people. . . . Now I have said all this in order that each one of the laity also may be aware that we may understand that we are all one body, having such differences among ourselves as members with members; and may not throw the whole upon the priests but ourselves also so care for the whole Church as for a body common to us."[10]

Others subsequently, for instance Saint Peter Damian, on the basis of the words of the Canon, "*we* offer," argues for the role of the whole Church.[11] Few have stressed the organic nature of the Eucharist more powerfully than Dix. Speaking precisely of the Offertory of the Mass he wrote:

> Irenaeus applied to the liturgical offertory the words of our Lord about the widow's mite—"That poor widow the Church casts in all her life (Lk 21:4) into the treasury of God" (*Adv. Haer.*, 4.18.2). Thus he stated epigrammatically the essential meaning of this part of the rite. Each communicant from the bishop to the newly confirmed gave *himself* under the forms of bread and wine to God, as God gives Himself to them under the same forms. In the united oblations of all her members the Body of Christ, the Church, gave herself to *become* the Body of Christ, the sacrament, in order that receiving again the symbol of herself now transformed and hallowed, she might be truly that which by nature she is, the Body of Christ, and each of her members members of Christ. In this self-giving the order of laity no less than that of the deacons or the high-priestly celebrant had its own indispensable function in the vital act of the Body. The layman brought the sacrifice of himself, of which he is the priest. The deacon, the

"servant" of the whole body, "presented" all together in the Person of
Christ, as Ignatius reminds us. The high-priest, the bishop "offered"
all together, for he alone can speak for the whole Body. In Christ, as His
Body, the Church is "accepted" by God "in the Beloved." Its sacrifice
of itself is taken up into His sacrifice of Himself. On this way of regarding
the matter the bishop can no more fulfil the layman's function for him
(he fulfils it on his own behalf by adding one *prosphora* for himself to the
people's offerings on the altar) than the layman can fulfil that of the bishop.

The whole rite was a true corporate offering by the Church in its
hierarchical completeness of the Church in its organic unity, so much so
that the penalty of mortal sin for members of every order was that they
were forbidden to "offer," each according to the liturgy of his own order.
The sinful layman was "forbidden to offer" (Cyprian, *Ep.* xvi. 14.), just as
the unfrocked deacon was forbidden to "present" . . . and the deposed
bishop was forbidden to celebrate (*prospherein*) where we should have said
"forbidden to receive communion."[12]

As noted earlier, this attribution to the people of the right to offer the
holy sacrifice constitutes a problem for those wedded to the one-act
model of sacrifice. Clark sees it as "the arrogation to the laity of
priestly power comparable with the power of order. What is of special
interest is that the exercise of this power is often ascribed to the
faithful's part in the *Offertory* of the Mass."[13] Pope Pius XII dealt with
the question in his encyclical *Mediator Dei*. Like Clark, he is careful
to distinguish the role of the laity and of the priest. "The fact, however,
that the faithful participate in the Eucharistic sacrifice does not mean
that they also are endowed with priestly power. It is very necessary
that you make this quite clear to your flocks."[14] He then develops the
special role of the priest in the sacrifice, in which he points out that
"we deem it necessary to recall that the priest acts for the people only
because he represents Jesus Christ, who is Head of all His members
and offers Himself in their stead. Hence, he goes to the altar as
minister of Christ, inferior to Christ but superior to the people. The
people, on the other hand, since they in no sense represent the divine
Redeemer and are not mediator between themselves and God, can
in no way possess the sacerdotal power."[15] The inference drawn from
these considerations is clearly stated. "But the conclusion that the
people offer the sacrifice with the priest himself is not based on the
fact that, being members of the Church no less than the priest himself,

they perform a visible liturgical rite; for this is the privilege only of the minister who has been divinely appointed to this office: rather, it is based on the fact that the people unite their hearts . . . with the prayers and intention of the priest, even of the High Priest Himself. . . ."[16] For Pope Pius XII, the laity cannot offer by any visible liturgical rite, but only by uniting themselves with the Eucharistic Prayer. The influence of the one-act model of sacrifice is clear to be seen. However, on the three-part model, the difficulty of finding distinct but complementary roles for priest and people disappears.

During his argument, Pope Pius XII remarked: "In this most important subject it is necessary, in order to avoid giving rise to a dangerous error, that we define the exact meaning of the word 'offer.'"[17] And therein precisely lies the solution to the problem. In the three-part model of sacrifice, as we have observed already, there are two distinct meanings to the word "offer." There is the primary offering of the offerer of the sacrifice, and there is the special offering reserved to the priest who mediates between the offerer and God. The offering of the sacrificial gift as symbolic of the gift of self belongs to the offerer, and the mediatorial offering belongs to the priest. Now, in the Eucharistic Sacrifice, as in the national sacrifices of Israel, the primary offerer is the whole people, priests and laity, and this is the offering of the sacrifice in which the laity participate by full right and "by [a] visible liturgical rite," the Offertory. When the Offertory is understood in its full meaning as an essential component of the sacrificial action, the role of the whole Church in offering the sacrifice stands out clearly, and there is no question of "the arrogation to the laity of priestly power comparable with the power of order." The issue does not arise. This offering, while being an essential part of the sacrifice, is quite clearly distinct from the mediatorial offering which belongs to the priest alone.

THE PRIVATE MASS

A related point to be tackled in this area is the issue of the private Mass. We dealt with this point earlier in defending the role of the Offertory in the private Mass, but there is the more serious theological question to be tackled. For a serious objection against the notion that the offering of the laity forms an essential part of the Eucharist is that it impugns the very validity of the private Mass. Clark formulates the objection as follows:

> A more modern scholar, Dom Gregory Dix, in a more subtle manner sees the liturgy as the act of the *organic* assembly of the Church, the Mystical Body of Christ, in which all participate according to their "order," with the implication that the participation of all "orders,"—priest, ministers and laity—is the true, Catholic manner of celebrating the Mass, and consequently Masses which are not celebrated with this *active* participation in some way fall short and do not correspond with primitive tradition. The further implication that the Mass is not the Mass without the presence and participation of the people is never explicitly drawn, but the writer is at pains to emphasise not merely that it is the assembly who offer the Mass but that it is a communal, if organic, act.[18]

The implication that Dix does not draw is the one that Clark is fearful of, "that the Mass is not the Mass without the presence and participation of the people." It is certainly true that the vision of the Mass which Dix presents, and that is being corroborated in this essay, emphasizes the fact that the Eucharist is the sacrifice of the whole Church, hierarchically assembled, and that "consequently Masses which are not celebrated with this *active* participation in some way fall short and do not correspond with primitive tradition." Now, this sense of the appropriateness of full participation by the whole Church has been present always in the Church. Even while the private Mass was accepted in practice during the second millennium in the West, it was never taken as ideal. It was always enjoined that there must be some participation beyond the priest alone. Right up until the 1917 Code at c. 813 § 1, it was forbidden for a priest to celebrate without an altar server, who could fulfil the roles of both people and deacon. This rule was only mitigated in the 1983 Code at c. 906, which lays down that "[a] priest may not celebrate the Eucharistic Sacrifice without the participation of at least one of the faithful, unless there is a good and reasonable cause for doing so." The real question at issue is that of validity, not appropriateness. Does the organic view of the sacrifice being advocated here imply "that the Mass is not the Mass without the presence and participation of the people"? There is no question that the private Mass is a less than ideal form of Eucharistic celebration, but is it valid?

Given the practice of the Roman Church for the last thousand years, the principle of its indefectibility demands that these Masses must be valid and we must see how. A communion sacrifice celebrated alone is undoubtedly an odd procedure. It is unimaginable that the Passover could be celebrated by a single man. Our Lord certainly couldn't have celebrated the Last Supper on his own. But when we are considering the Eucharist different considerations have to be invoked. The communion sacrifice in this case is a sacramental sacrifice, and is the sacrifice of the whole Church, the whole People of God, and they obviously cannot all be present at any given celebration. In any Eucharist, the congregation is representative of the whole Church, which is always the one offering the sacrifice. Now, must there be a quorum? Must there be present a specified number of lay people together with the priest to ensure the validity of the sacrifice? The Canon Law until 1983 specified that there must be at least one, and even still the complete absence of any other Christian is deemed to be exceptional. Now, with the priest by himself, can the full reality of the three-part sacrificial action be effected? In fact it can. The important point is that it is the whole People who are the primary offerers of the sacrifice, and the priest is a member of the People just as are the laity. It is not the laity who are the primary offerers, but the whole People, priest and laity together. The priest alone can be a legitimate primary offerer of the sacrifice even in the absence of the laity. He is not offering simply on his own behalf, he is offering on behalf of the whole Church, *in persona Ecclesiae.* As was pointed out earlier, it is clearly understood that when the priest is offering the bread and wine, he is not offering it as his own, but as the property of the Church. The fact that every Mass is in principle available of a Mass stipend makes that point clear. It is implied by the fact that the priest always says "We offer" during the Eucharistic Prayer, making clear that he is making the offering on behalf of the people, even if they have had no active part in its ritual presentation, and even if they are not present at all. This is the background to the teaching of Pope Pius XII: "Moreover, this sacrifice, necessarily and of its very nature, has always and everywhere the character of a public and social act, inasmuch as he who offers it acts in the name of Christ and of the faithful, whose Head is the divine Redeemer, and he offers it to God for the holy catholic Church, and for the living and the dead. This is undoubtedly so, whether the faithful are present . . . or are not present. . . ."[19] So, we conclude that the practice in the Western Church of the private Mass does not constitute a norm for the liturgy, and that the organic vision of the Eucharistic Sacrifice as, in principle, an act of the whole Church, hierarchically assembled, stands firm in spite of it.

The Active Participation of the Faithful

Yet another related question is that of the active participation of the faithful in the Eucharistic liturgy, which is the goal of the reform of the liturgy mandated by the Second Vatican Council (*Sacrosanctum Concilium*, 14). A proper understanding of sacrifice has a very important contribution to make to this issue. Let us begin our consideration of this aspect by listening to a comment by Yerkes about a fundamental aspect of the traditional understanding of sacrifice.

> In modern English two groups of verbs are related to worship. A person may be described as (1) saying or reading or singing, or (2) performing or conducting or celebrating a religious service. In both instances the verb describes the action of a single person, or of a very small group of persons. Others who may be present are spectators or auditors who attend or watch or hear the service, which may be perfectly transmitted by radio or television. . . . We have become so accustomed to this method of thinking that we do not always realise the radically different concept of worship which obtained among ancient Greeks. Verbs of saying and performing and hearing and seeing were proper for pageantry and play; they had no place in descriptions of a thusia, for which the only adequate verbs were those of group action in which every member had a part; none was a mere spectator or auditor.[20]

So, if one is truly sacrificing, one is of necessity active. And Dix makes the same point at considerable length in relation to Christian sacrifice. He points out that:

> . . . the general conception . . . of what the Eucharist fundamentally is . . . [is] something which is *said*, to which is attached an action, the act of communion. . . . regards this, of course, as an essential constituent part of the whole, but it is nevertheless something attached to the "saying," and rather as a consequence than as a climax. The conception before the fourth century and in the New Testament is almost the reverse of this. It regards the rite as primarily something *done*, of which what is said is only

one incidental constituent part, though of course an essential one. . . .
We all find it easy and natural to use such phrases as, of the clergy, *"saying*
Mass," and of the laity, *"hearing* Mass" . . . The ancients on the contrary
habitually spoke of *"doing* the Eucharist," *"performing* the mysteries,"
"making the synaxis," *"doing* the offering." And there is a further contrast,
that while our language implies a certain difference between the functions
of the clergy and the laity, *"saying"* and *"hearing* Mass," the ancients used
all their active language about "doing" the liturgy quite indifferently of laity
and clergy alike. The irreplaceable function of the celebrant, his "special
liturgy," was to "make" the prayer; just as the irreplaceable function of the
deacon or the people was to *do* something else which the celebrant did not
do. There was difference of function but no distinction in kind between
the activities of the different orders in the worship of the whole Church.[21]

He reminds us of something whose background we have followed
earlier, that "[i]t was in the Latin middle ages that the Eucharist
became for the first time essentially something 'said' rather than something 'done' (the East has never accepted such a change),"[22] and draws
his conclusion:

The first main distinction, then, which we have to bear in mind, is that the
apostolic and primitive Church regarded the Eucharist as primarily an
action, something "done," not something "said"; and that it had a clear and
unhesitating grasp of the fact that this action was *corporate*, the united joint
action of the whole Church and not of the celebrant only. The prayer
which the celebrant "said" was not the predominant thing in the rite. It
took its place alongside the "special liturgies" of each of the other "orders,"
as one essential in the corporate worshipful act of the whole Church, even
as the most important essential, but to the exclusion of the essential
character of the others.[23]

And what is it that the people principally "do" in offering a sacrifice?
We have already seen Dix making clear that the people's part in the
offering of a sacrifice is precisely the Offertory. This point has been well
made more recently by a Catholic commentator on the liturgy. He is
speaking of the history of the Offertory, but in the context of our discussion we can understand him to be speaking of the reality of the sacrifice.

All of these gifts (those used specifically at the celebration of the Eucharist,
as well as those destined for the support of the clergy and for the works of
charity of the congregation) were looked upon as being a contribution
to the sacrifice; and in the offering of these gifts one could see how each

member of the congregation expressed concretely his intention of taking
an active part in the sacrifice, and of making an offering of his very self.
The fact that most of the oblations, in an age which was accustomed
to trade in kind, were products of the labour of people's own hands served
to enhance the symbolism of the offertory gift in the mind of the individual worshipper. For in his gift at the offertory, he gave something of his
own substance, something fundamental to his very existence and by doing
this represented the giving of himself. The practical effect of such
oblations was at one and the same time to provide an economic foundation
for the existence of the clergy and of the Church's work of charity; the
clergy, like the poor, lived so to speak "from the altar"; and the Eucharistic
sacrifice was at the same time the very source of the charitable activity
of Christians.[24]

Here is the principal meaning of the active participation of the people
in a sacrifice, the offering of their gifts as symbolic of the offering of
their lives to God.[25] And not alone do the gifts of bread and wine become
the Body and Blood of Christ, but the gifts in kind become the
sustenance of the Church, her ministers and her poor. This is the
fundamental meaning of active participation which has been obscured
for centuries, as Klauser goes on to relate.

This obligation to take part in the offertory procession was enforced by
many synods right up into the eleventh century; then the bishop's admoni-
tions gradually ceased, a clear sign that this institution was nearing its total
eclipse. Its inability to survive is understandably connected to a certain
extent with the fact that since the ninth century, primarily (we presume)
under the influence of Old Testament texts, the use of unleavened bread at
the celebration of the Eucharist in the West became the general custom;
the most important contribution to the sacrifice made by the faithful, the
bread that they baked at home, became from this period onwards no
longer usable as bread for the Eucharist. Even more important, however,
was the fact that the faithful could now no longer take a personal part in
the private Mass, now far and away the most widespread form of the
Eucharistic service. In place of the gifts which they had formerly presented
as offerings at the Mass, there was gradually substituted the "Mass
stipend" which to begin with understandably consisted of gifts "in kind,"
but later simply money, by means of which the faithful claimed the right
to have a Mass celebrated privately for themselves and for their own
personal intentions.[26]

With Empty Hands?

At this point, something must be said about the question of our
"offering" anything at all in the Eucharist, which seems to be a fundamental problem in this whole matter. The Lutheran polemic against
the Offertory must have been springing from some deep source, for it
seems to have met with eventual success. The turn away from the
Offertory in the Western Church since the turn of the first millennium
seems to indicate a source deep in the Western psyche. If our
Eucharistic piety is to be based on the reality of the sacrifice, the role
of the Offertory must be properly conceived and then made effective
in practice. It is not only among Protestants that it is taken for granted
that we must come before God "with empty hands." It is a commonplace of Catholic liturgists when dealing with the Offertory to rule out
of court any suggestion that we bring a gift to God. "What in any case
needs to be avoided is any suggestion that we have anything to give to
God," says one, making the point as something quite taken for
granted.[27] Of course, there is an important truth being affirmed here.
"What have you that you have not received?" (1 Corinthians 4:7). All
that we have is a gift from God. And yet the other side of the coin is
also of fundamental importance. God's greatest gift to us is the capability
of offering Him gifts in return for His goodness to us. It was a
fundamental norm of Old Testament piety that "No one shall appear
before Me empty-handed" (Exodus 23:15). The bringing of a gift
is at the heart of sacrifice. One must bring something of one's own to
God. Gayford makes the point for the Old Testament sacrifices. "The
thing offered must be the personal property of the sacrificer: 'of thy
flock,' 'of the fruit of thy ground' (see, for example, Exodus 22:29, 23:16;
Leviticus 1:2, 2:14; Deuteronomy 12:6, 16:10, etc.). . . . Now this
means that it is not the intrinsic value of the gift that God regards but
its cost to the giver. . . *It is the degree of self-sacrifice involved in the gift
that makes it precious in His eyes;* in other words, all Sacrifice, so far as it
is worth anything in the sight of God, is self-sacrifice."[28] And this is
the sense of the Christian tradition also, as made clear by Saint Irenaeus.

> It is not, therefore, on account of His needing anything that He wishes
> us to do these things, but in order to give thanks to His majesty and
> sanctify His gift; . . . Although he does not need it, then, he nonetheless
> desires that we do it for our sake so that we will not remain bereft of fruit.

This is why the very same Word gave the people the commandment
to make offerings (προσφορὰς), not because He needs them, but so that
we should in that way learn to serve God. He therefore desires from us
that we should always unceasingly offer the gift (προσφέρειν τὸ δῶρόν)
on the altar. The real altar, however, is heaven, which is the goal of all our
prayers and offerings.[29]

The fact is that the Offertory is a joint action of God and the offerer.
The new Offertory prayers make the point clearly that it is through
the goodness of God that we have our gifts to offer which are "fruit of
the earth and work of human hands." It is clear that the eclipse of the
Offertory in the Western liturgy is a very serious loss to the Church.
and if the present understanding of the matter is correct, this trend
must be completely reversed. The old laws insisting that Christians
"offer" the Holy Sacrifice need to restored. They continued to be recalled
in the Western Church until the eleventh century, and it was only
when the liturgy of the Mass began its decay that the legal situation
changed. The change is clear in the important universal law introduced by Pope Innocent III at the Fourth Lateran Council in 1215,
imposing annual Communion on all the faithful. The decree laid
down that the faithful should "reverently receive" the sacrament of the
Eucharist at least once a year. The change in the understanding of the
Eucharist is clear in this choice of the word "receive." Instead of being
a sacrifice which one "offers," the Eucharist has become the Body
and Blood of Christ which one "receives." By this time, the understanding of the sacrifice has already disappeared and it must be restored
if the Eucharist is to be celebrated as Christ intended. The recent
reform of the liturgy has gone a long way in restoring the ancient
tradition. The new General Instruction of the Roman Missal
lays down: "It is fitting for the faithful's participation to be expressed
by their presenting both the bread and wine for the celebration of
the Eucharist and other gifts to meet the needs of the Church and of
the poor."[30] This is a start, no doubt, but if the understanding of
sacrifice being presented here is correct, it is more than simply "fitting"
that the faithful should actually "offer" sacrifice in the full sense. If this
understanding is to be recovered in practice, the Offertory must be
fully restored.

THE SACRAMENTAL SACRIFICE

We come, then, to the last stage of our investigation when we examine the relationship between the Eucharist and the Sacrifice of the Cross. We began by making the case for the position that the Eucharist is a sacrifice of bread and wine that is a sacrament of the Sacrifice of the Cross. We then presented a model of sacrifice drawn from the experience of the Old Testament, which sees a sacrifice as a three-part event made up of an offertory, the priestly mediation, and the sacred meal. Next, this model was compared with the Eucharist and it was concluded that the Eucharist also follows this three-part model, being made up of the Offertory, the Eucharistic Prayer, and Communion. This three-part model was then applied to the Sacrifice of the Cross, and the same three-part structure was verified there, where the Passion and death of the Lord constituted the offertory of the sacrifice, his intercession at the right hand of the Father the priestly mediation, and the banquet of eternal life the sacred meal. The last step that we must now take is to match the two sacrifices and see how the three parts of each are symbolically related to the corresponding parts of the other.

Of course, this matching of the Eucharist with Christ's Sacrifice has been going on throughout Christian tradition, and different approaches have been taken at different times. The dominant approach in Western theology for many centuries has been that based on the one-act model of sacrifice of which we have had occasion often to speak. On this model, the Sacrifice of the Cross, as the name implies, is constituted mainly by Christ's death on the Cross and so the Eucharist is understood to be a symbolic representation of that death. We can take Saint Thomas as representative of this approach. Francis Clark summarizes his view. "The Eucharist, St Thomas explains, is the representative image of the bloody immolation of Christ on Calvary; it is itself a sacrifice and an oblation containing the same victim really present; it is not a different sacrifice from Calvary; in it Christ, now glorious and impassible, can suffer no more; he offers himself at the altar through the instrumentality of the priests of his Church; the propitiatory effects of his passion flow to men through the Mass, for the remission of sins and for the welfare of the living and the dead."[31] And this view of the matter has acquired a certain official status in *Mediator Dei,* in which Pope Pius XII teaches that "[o]n the altar . . . the shedding of his blood is impossible; still, according to the plan of divine wisdom, the sacrifice of our Redeemer is shown forth in an admirable manner, by external signs which are symbols of his death. For by 'transubstantiation' of bread into the body of Christ and of wine into his blood, his body and blood are both really present; now the Eucharistic species under which he is present, symbolise the actual separation of his body and blood."[32]

However, when we look at the Christian tradition as a whole, this almost exclusive focus on the Cross in relation to the Eucharist is a comparative novelty, and the primary evidence here is the liturgy itself. Hicks makes the point well.

> What is decisive as regards the general trend of sacrificial language is the fact that for the first four or five centuries the range of the sacrificial idea is as wide as possible. It was in this period that the main lines, as well as much of the wording, of the Liturgies, were fixed. And whatever may have been the later adventures in interpretation of Eucharistic theology, or in experience of Eucharistic devotion, the liturgies survive as unmistakable evidence of the earlier conceptions. It is not until we come to Liturgies drawn up at the time of the Reformation that, as in the Consecration Prayer of the second English Prayer Book, first issued in 1552, the commemoration of our Lord's redeeming work is limited to His death. That, for all its simplicity, was a medievalist conception. It is not primitive. Every primitive consecration prayer in every part of the Christian world; every Eastern liturgy, earlier or later; every form of the Canon in the Western Mass, including the present Roman Canon, preserves the width of the original outlook. The redeeming work of Christ is not His Death only, but also His Resurrection, and His Ascension, or, as the latter is often amplified, His Ascension and His Session at the right hand of God.[33]

The proposal to be made here is that this parallel based on the one-act model of sacrifice is inadequate and that, on the three-part model of sacrifice, a part for part matching of the two sacrifices reveals a quite different structure of the symbolic relationship between the sacramental sacrifice of the Eucharist and reality signified and made real, the universal Sacrifice of Christ. We have verified the three-part model of sacrifice in the Eucharist and in Christ's Sacrifice on the Cross and in heaven. It remains now to relate the one to the other, seeing how the parts of the Eucharist correspond to the parts of Christ's Sacrifice. The three parts are the offertory, the priestly mediation, and the meal.

In the Eucharist there corresponds the Offertory, the Eucharistic Prayer, and Communion. In Christ's Sacrifice there corresponds the Cross, Christ's intercession at the right hand of the Father, and the banquet of eternal life. The matching of the two, therefore, leads to the conclusion that the Offertory of the Eucharist corresponds to the Passion and death of the Lord, the Eucharistic Prayer corresponds to Christ's intercession at the Father's right hand, and Communion corresponds to the banquet of eternal life. There are two complete sacrifices and one is the sacrament of the other.

The Offertory

On this view of the relationship between the Eucharist and Christ's Sacrifice, a new perspective on the fundamental importance of the Offertory in the structure of the Mass comes to light, for, as opposed to the parallel in the one-act model of sacrifice, it is the Offertory which corresponds to the Cross in Christ's Sacrifice, and not the Eucharistic Prayer. And this understanding fits remarkably with some of the strange and beautiful aspects of the Eastern liturgy which have ever puzzled the liturgists and the theologians. One description of the Byzantine Offertory runs as follows.

> In the evolved Byzantine rite the practice and symbolism of the Offertory were developed. In a ceremony called the Prothesis that takes place before the Liturgy of the Word, the offerings are prepared on a table apart. With the "Sacred Lance" the priest makes five incisions in the bread to signify the sacred wounds. At one point he gives the order: "Perform the sacrifice, deacon," whereupon the deacon makes a cross-shaped cut in the bread. After the Liturgy of the Word, the ceremonious Great Entry takes place while the priest says prayers recalling our Lord's burial.[34]

The meaning of the symbolism being evoked is spelled out in a particular way by Theodore of Mopsuestia.[35]

> By means of the signs we must see Christ now being led away to His passion and again later when He is stretched out on the altar to be immolated for us. When the offering which is about to be presented is brought out in the sacred vessels, on the patens and in the chalice, you must imagine that Christ our Lord is being led out to His passion.[36] . . . They bring up the bread and place it on the holy altar to complete the representation of the passion. So from now on we should consider that Christ has already

undergone the passion and is now placed on the altar as if in a tomb.[37] . . .
When we see the offering on the altar like a body laid in a tomb, recollection
takes hold of all present because of the dread rites that are performed.
So they are obliged with recollection and fear to watch what is being done,
because at this moment, through the awesome liturgy as it is performed
according to the priestly rules, Christ our Lord is to rise from the dead,
proclaiming to all a share in His sublime blessings. This is why in the offering we recall our Lord's death: it is the proclamation of the resurrection
and the sublime blessings.[38]

It is clear that the parallelism between the Offertory and the Cross
demanded by the three-part model of sacrifice is what Theodore of
Mopsuestia has in mind, and what the Eastern liturgy is symbolizing.
This is surely a remarkable confirmation of the perspective opened
up by the three-part model. And there is even a hint of the same
vision in one aspect of the Western liturgical tradition, in our calling
the unconsecrated bread "hosts." As Jungmann points out: "The term
we now employ for the wafers destined for the Eucharist is the
proleptic expression 'hosts.' The word *hostia* was originally used only
for a living thing, the sacrificial victim that was 'slaughtered' (*hostio* =
ferio, I strike, I kill). It could therefore be understood in the first
instance only of Christ, who had become for us a *hostia* (cf. Eph. 5:2),
a sacrificial Lamb. . . . The exact parallel . . . is found in the Byzantine
liturgy where the piece of bread selected in the *proskomide* and
destined for the consecration is called the 'Lamb.'"[39] Pius Parsch, in
his analysis of the Eucharistic liturgy, had already noted this fundamental link between the Offertory and the Cross. "This entrance into
the sacrifice of the Lord was beautifully expressed in the Offertory
procession; the faithful brought to the altar their gifts, which symbolized their own selves. Thus they laid themselves upon the altar of
sacrifice, to die with Christ in sacrifice. This indeed is the most profound significance of the Offertory—our entering into the sacrificial
death of Christ."[40]

And the mystery does not end there. Dix tells us further that
during the Great Entrance "the people offer adoration to the elements
borne by before their eyes, while the choir sings the *Cherubikon*, a
hymn composed in the later sixth century. . . . The profound reverence
and actual worship rendered to the unconsecrated elements during this
procession have been a source of embarrassment to Eastern theologians,

and a standing puzzle to liturgists. . . ."[41] In fact, we are told that at one stage "the patriarch of Constantinople, St Eutychius, opposed the custom (which was then an innovation) of celebrating the 'King of Glory'" at the moment of this procession, "before the invocation of the pontiff has brought about the consecration of the bread and chalice, which were the objects of this honor. His protest had no effect. The 'great entrance' remained unchanged with the Gregorian Armenians, who always sing at this point: 'Open up, eternal gates, and the King of Glory will enter' (Psalm 24), and with the Byzantines, who accompany it with the marvelous *Cherubikon*. This explains the anticipatory nature of certain attitudes and formulas which seem strange to Westerners, who reserve them for the real presence."[42] The Eastern sense of the liturgy understands that the transubstantiation of the elements has already taken place as soon as the Offertory begins. This would also fit with the implications of the three-part model, where it is not simply the bread and wine that are transubstantiated into the Body and Blood of Christ, but the whole communion sacrifice of bread and wine is transubstantiated into Christ's Universal Sacrifice. From this it would follow that Christ our Lord is really and truly present during the Offertory, symbolically on the Way of the Cross to his Passion and Death.

All this gives an alternative interpretation to an affirmation of Saint Cyprian which is considered to be at the basis of the whole Western approach to the Eucharistic Sacrifice. Dix tells that "for Cyprian the whole question of *how* the Eucharist is constituted a sacrifice is as clear-cut and completely settled as it is for a post-Tridentine theologian: 'Since we make mention of His passion in all our sacrifices, *for the passion is the Lord's sacrifice which we offer*, we ought to do nothing else than what He did (at the Last Supper).'"[43] Now, Dix presumes here that Cyprian's likeness of the Passion to the sacrifice that we offer is a reference to the Eucharist as a whole. However, it is just as likely, and, indeed, even more probable that Cyprian had precisely the Offertory in mind, and this for a number of reasons. In the first place, the whole of Epistle 53 is on the subject of the Offertory in particular. As we noticed already, the occasion was the abuse of offering water alone rather than wine mixed with water, and Cyprian's response was to insist that we do as the Lord did in his offering. Furthermore, at this early stage, the word "sacrifice" would still have been understood as primarily referring to the gift offered rather than to the liturgical rite as a whole. As mentioned already, this was the original scriptural usage and it remained normal in the tradition for centuries. So, we suggest that Cyprian's seminal remark making the link between the Eucharist and the Cross was referring specifically to the Offertory, and thus in perfect harmony with the understanding of the sacrifice we have observed in the East.

These different considerations give an even greater significance to the Offertory, which we have already seen to be essential to the sacrificial action. If it is correct to conclude from what we have seen that it is the Offertory that is the symbolic representation of the Cross in the Eucharist, then the significance of the Offertory is great indeed. The whole spirituality of self-offering that is dominant in the understanding of the Eucharist as sacrifice is now focused on the Offertory. It is precisely in the Offertory that the Church offers itself in union with Christ to the Father. This is the primary meaning of the word "offer" and it is the action of the whole Church, priest and laity. In the one-act model, this primary meaning of offering is focused on the priest and then transferred to the laity by their spiritual cooperation with the priest's offering in the person of Christ. On this understanding, it is the whole Church that makes this primary offering in the person of Christ, and the priest's mediatorial offering comes after, and to it we now turn.

The Eucharistic Prayer

We come now to the second act of the Eucharistic sacrifice, the Eucharistic Prayer. On the model being proposed, it corresponds to the priestly mediation of Christ's Universal Sacrifice which is his intercession at the Father's right hand. The major point here in matching the two is that the three-part model of sacrifice demands that the Eucharistic Prayer takes place symbolically in heaven. If the Offertory is symbolic of Christ's death on the Cross, then the priestly mediation which follows must be in heaven, and again the evidence of the liturgy corroborates this conclusion. According to Hicks: "The evidence of the liturgies is decisive. . . . The outward part of the worship of the Church is on earth, expressed in human words, and in earthly acts. But its inward, unseen, part is in heaven. It is the worship of heaven in

which the Church on earth joins: hearts are lifted up to the throne
of God; the angels are part of the worshipping throng; and the angelic
hymn, the Holy, Holy, Holy, is the summary of the praise alike of
earth and of heaven."[44]

The Eucharistic Prayer begins in every liturgy with the
preface and the *Sanctus,* in which the heavenly dimension is made
quite clear by always recalling that we are joining our worship to that
of the angels and saints in heaven. Other small points of the Western
liturgy point in the same direction. In the Roman Canon, there is
the prayer where we ask that "your angel would take this sacrifice
to your altar in heaven," and that we would receive from "this altar" (in
heaven) the Body and Blood of Christ. One commentator interprets
the "secret" prayer of the old Roman liturgy in just this sense. "At Rome
in the time of *Ordo I,* the Eucharistic Prayer could still be heard by the
congregation. . . . But when the same liturgy was celebrated in
Frankish territory, probably in the second half of the ninth century, the
relevant *Ordo* adds: 'in a low voice' (*tacito intrat in canonem*). The formula
suggests the high priest entering alone into the Holy of Holies. . . .
The trend to silence affected other prayers as well. Thus the Roman
prayer 'over the gifts' acquired the name 'Secret.'"[45] Not unexpectedly,
however, it is again in the East that the point is made most dramatically.

> In most present-day Eastern churches the sanctuary is separated from
> the nave by an opaque partition that is decorated with icons in accordance
> with strict rules—the "iconostasis." . . . A central door, which remains
> shut during a large part of the liturgy, and two side doors provide for
> communication between the sanctuary and the rest of the building. This
> arrangement appeared only at the end of the fourteenth century in the
> Slavic countries and spread from there throughout the Churches of the
> Levant. . . . The only explanation for its success is that it was in harmony
> with a conception of the liturgical celebration that was familiar to the
> Eastern faithful. As early as the eighth century we find the space around
> the altar being described as the "Holy of Holies" and therefore "accessible
> only to priests." . . . The deacons, whose ministry is compared to that
> of the angels, spend part of their time within the sanctuary, assisting the
> celebrant, and part of the time outside, where they lead the faithful in
> prayer. . . . The deacons ascend and descend the ladder of Jacob, as it
> were, and act as link between the faithful and the image of heaven that is
> the sanctuary.[46]

Hicks's interpretation is surely exact. "In the East . . . the altar is shut off from the people, except at the moments when the Royal Doors are opened, by the iconostasis, or screen. . . . the Altar, . . . the sanctuary—the whole space within the screen—*is* symbolically Heaven. . . ."[47] And the Fathers concur, for example, Saint Irenaeus. "Thus is it, therefore, also His will that we, too, should offer a gift at the altar, frequently and without intermission. The altar, then, is in heaven (for towards that place are our prayers and oblations directed); the temple likewise, as John says in the Apocalypse, 'And the temple of God was opened': the tabernacle also: 'For, behold,' he says, 'the tabernacle of God, in which He will dwell with men.'"[48] And Theodore of Mopsuestia is again of interest.

> Every time, then, there is performed the liturgy of this awesome sacrifice, which is the clear image of the heavenly realities, we should imagine that we are in heaven. Faith enables us to picture in our minds the heavenly realities, as we remind ourselves that the same Christ who is in heaven, who died for us, rose again and ascended to heaven, is now being immolated under these symbols. So when faith enables our eyes to contemplate the commemoration that takes place now, we are brought again to see His death, resurrection and ascension, which have already taken place for our sake.[49]

We have, then, yet another liturgical confirmation of the implications of the three-part model of sacrifice, where the model demands that the Eucharistic Prayer be symbolically in heaven and the liturgy agrees.

The parallel gives another implication as well which provides the meaning of the mediatorial offering of the priest. Since the Eucharistic Prayer corresponds to Christ's heavenly intercession, the implication follows that the priest's "offering" is principally prayer, and prayer of intercession in particular. Again the liturgy confirms this expectation. The Eucharistic Prayer is a prayer of praise and a memorial of Christ's Sacrifice, but it is also full of intercession, intercession for the whole Church. So, the offering of the priest in the Eucharistic Prayer is not the primary offering of the sacrifice, the gift of self that corresponds to Christ's gift of himself to death on the Cross. That privilege belongs to the Offertory, which is the act of the whole People, priest and laity together. The priest's specific offering in the Eucharistic

Prayer is the mediatorial offering of prayer to God for the intentions of the whole Church offering the sacrifice.

Communion

According to the parallelism between the Eucharistic sacrifice and the Universal Sacrifice, the third part of the Eucharist, Communion, corresponds to the third part of Christ's Sacrifice, the banquet of eternal life. Symbolically, therefore, we are still in heaven and Christ is sharing his Body and Blood with us in the sacred meal that is the culmination of the sacrifice. In the basic structure of the Eucharist, this part corresponds to the "breaking of the bread," and in this phrase, which was the first name for the Eucharist in Christian tradition, the direct link to the resurrected life of Jesus can be discerned. "The Breaking of Bread is linked to the meals the Apostles shared with the risen Christ."[50] This aspect of sharing food with Jesus after his Resurrection was so important that "St. Peter characterises the witnesses of the Resurrection as those who 'did eat and drink with Him after He arose again from the dead' (Acts 10:41)."[51] What is significant in the early Church's choice of this name for the Eucharist is the clear primary emphasis placed on the meal as the culminating act of the sacrifice. This fits with the understanding of sacrifice involved in meal theory, so that when the early Christians thought of the Eucharist, thought of the Christian sacrifice, what they had in mind was the meal. And it was understood as a meal shared with the living, resurrected Christ, and therefore symbolically in heaven. This understanding can be seen in the phrase that introduces the Communion in the current Eucharistic liturgy: "Blessed are those who are called to his supper." The reference here is to Revelation 19:9: "Blessed are those who are called to the marriage supper of the Lamb," and that supper is the banquet of eternal life.

And so the sacramental sacrifice is complete. In the Eucharist the complete Sacrifice of Christ is symbolized and made real. If we take into account the preceding Liturgy of the Word, the full Eucharistic liturgy re-enacts the fullness of the Incarnation. Christ enters the world in the Entrance Rite, we become his disciples in the Penitential Rite or the Renewal of Baptism, and the Liturgy of the Word symbolizes the public life of the Lord. The Eucharist proper as we have outlined it renews the fullness of his sacrifice, the Offertory representing the Passion and death of Jesus, and the Eucharistic Prayer and Communion symbolizing and realizing his ongoing saving work in heaven, his intercession at God's right hand, and the banquet of eternal life. Now, surely this wide perspective is more satisfactory than the narrow focus of the whole significance on the Cross alone that is characteristic of the one-act model of sacrifice which has been dominant for so long. On this three-part model of sacrifice, the Cross retains its central place, but is now seen as having its role in a bigger reality. It is now seen to be a means to an end, the focus no longer on death but on the life it ushers in. When sacrifice is seen to be the overall context of Christ's saving work, and the three-part model is accepted, then the relationship between the Cross and the Resurrection is clear. The sacrifice is the sacred meal, and the death is an essential means to its preparation. It is not the tragic loss of life that holds center stage, but the releasing of new life to be shared in the banquet of eternal life. It turns out then, that while retaining the central role of the Cross in the Eucharist, the liturgy is not overcast with the shadow of death, but it is seen to be the celebration of life and joy which the Lord intended.

CONCLUSION

Our journey is now completed. We began by arguing that a coherent and generally accepted notion of sacrifice is essential for Catholic theology. We based this on the teaching of the Church, formulated clearly at the Council of Trent, that the Eucharist is a true and proper sacrifice of bread and wine. We next presented the structure of the three-part model of sacrifice discerned in the sacrifices of the ancient world in general and in Israel in particular by F. C. Gayford and R. K. Yerkes. We argued that, when the essential place of the Offertory in the Eucharist is properly appreciated, then the three-part model of sacrifice is quite obviously verified there. We then applied the three-part model to the Sacrifice of the Cross and found that some surprising results emerged which, while being strange to us who have been formed on the one-act model of sacrifice, turned out be part of the Church's tradition and to make excellent sense at the same time. As a last step in the process, we applied the results achieved to the Eucharist both as a natural and a sacramental sacrifice. In this section we found that some long-standing difficulties of Eucharistic theology resolved themselves quite expeditiously on the presuppositions of the three-part model, and that some apparent anomalies of the Eucharistic liturgy found a context in which they fitted perfectly. Obviously, not everything has been said. What has been presented is yet another attempt to find a notion of sacrifice that fits all the essential criteria required to make it acceptable to the faith of the Church. However, it is the conviction of the present writer that enough has been said to justify the contention that this three-part model of sacrifice must be considered a serious candidate for the essential notion of sacrifice which the Church is seeking.

---

1. CT VI, 350.27–30.

2. CT VII, I, 389.8–10.

3. Ep. 63 *Cyprianus Caecilio fratri S.*, IV, § 1, CCL, III C, p. 392.40–1.

4. Augustine, Ep. 98 *Bonifatio episcopo*, § 9; CSEL 34, 2, 530, 21–531, 5; PL 33, 363.

5. Vonier, *A Key to the Doctrine of the Eucharist*, 87.

6. *Confessio Fidei* IV, 1, PL 101, 1087. (Reference in DTC X, I , 1034.)

7. "Non ergo solum panem et vinum quae corporaliter videntur, sed et . . . Verbum et Filium Dei offert sancta Ecclesia." (*De dev. Off.*, l. II, c. 2, PL 170, 34.) (Reference in DTC X, I, 1038.)

8. *panis deifer*, PL 170, 35C, 40C.

9. S. Moore, "The Theology of the Mass and the Liturgical Datum," *The Downside Review* 69 (1951) 31–44, at p. 31.

10. *Hom. 18 in 2 Cor.*, § 3. PG 61, 257; (English translation in LNPNF, 12, 365–366).

11. *Liber qui dicitur Dominus vobiscum*, 8; PL 145, 237C–238B; licet ab uno specialiter offerri sacerdote videatur, 237D.

12. Dix, *The Shape of the Liturgy*, 117.

13. Clark, "The Function of the Offertory Rite in the Mass," 311.

14. *Mediator Dei*, AAS 39 (1947) 553;§ 82. In *The Papal Encyclicals 1939–1958*, Claudia Carlen, IHM, ed. (Wilmington: McGrath, 1981), 133.

15. Ibid. AAS 39 (1947) 553 (DS 3850); § 84. Carlen, 134.

16. Ibid., AAS 39 (1947) 556; § 93. Carlen, 135.

17. Ibid., AAS 39 (1947) 555; § 92. Carlen, 134.

18. Clark, "The Function of the Offertory Rite in the Mass," 311.

19. *Mediator Dei*, 96. AAS 39 (1947) 557. Carlen, 135.

20. Yerkes, *Sacrifice in Greek and Roman Religions and Early Judaism*, 95–96.

21. Dix, *The Shape of the Liturgy*, 12.

22. Ibid., 13.

23. Ibid., 15.

24. Theodor Klauser, *A Short History of the Western Liturgy* (Oxford: Oxford University Press, 1979), 109.

25. One early twentieth-century liturgist was already aware of this significance. Pius Parsch advocated the re-introduction of the Offertory procession on the basis that the "essence of the Offertory . . . is the Offertory procession." *The Liturgy of the Mass* (St. Louis: Herder, 1936), 153.

26. Klauser, *A Short History of the Western Liturgy*, 110.

27. J. D. Crichton, *Christian Celebration: The Mass* (London: Geoffrey Chapman, 1971), 83.

28. Gayford, *Sacrifice and the Priesthood*, 18.

29. *Adversus Haereses* IV, 18, 6; PG 7, 1029; SC 100, 614–615, 135ss.

30. *Institutio Generalis Missalis Romani* (2000), § 140.

31. Clark, "The Function of the Offertory Rite in the Mass," 77–78.

32. *Mediator Dei*, AAS 39 (1947) 548, § 70. Carlen, 131.

33. Hicks, *The Fullness of Sacrifice*, 281.

34. Edward Yarnold, sj, *The Awe-Inspiring Rites of Initiation*, 2nd ed. (Edinburgh: T. & T. Clark, 1994), p. 43.

35. Theodore of Mopsuestia: Baptismal Homily IV; in Yarnold, *The Awe-Inspiring Rites of Initiation*, 216ff.

36. Ibid. § 25, p. 216.

37. Ibid.§ 26, p. 217.

38. Ibid.§ 29, p. 218–219.

39. Jungmann, *The Mass of the Roman Rite*, Vol. 2, 37.

40. Parsch, *The Liturgy of the Mass* (St. Louis: Herder, 1936), 163.

41. Dix, *The Shape of the Liturgy*, 285.

42. Robert Cabié, et al., ed. *The Church at Prayer: Vol. 2, The Eucharist* (Shannon: Irish University Press, 1973); N. M. Denis-Boulet, "The Offertory," 113–130, at 116–117.

43. Dix, *The Shape of the Liturgy*, 115. The Cyprianic reference is to *Ep.*, lxiii, 17.

44. Hicks, *The Fullness of Sacrifice*, 282.

45. Robert Cabié, *The Church at Prayer: Vol. 2, The Eucharist* (Collegeville: The Liturgical Press, 1986), 133.

46. Ibid., 143.

47. Hicks, *The Fullness of Sacrifice*, 344–345.

48. *Adversus Haereses*, IV, 18, 6.; sc 100, 614–615

49. Baptismal Homily IV, § 20, Yarnold, *The Awe-Inspiring Rites of Initiation*, 213.

50. Durrwell, *The Resurrection*, 320, referring to O. Cullmann, *Rev. Hist. Phil. Rel.*, 1936, 1–22.

51. Ibid.